The Transfiguration
of Jesus

Marshall

_2000_

The Transfiguration of Jesus

ROB MARSHALL

Foreword by Rowan Williams

DARTON · LONGMAN + TODD

First published 1994 by
Darton, Longman and Todd Ltd
1 Spencer Court
140–142 Wandsworth High Street
London SW18 4JJ

ISBN 0–232–52028–3

A catalogue record for this book is available
from the British Library

Acknowledgements

Lion Publishing for permission to reproduce the poem
'Transfiguration' by Kevin Mills, originally published
in *100 Contemporary Christian Poets*, quoted on p. 7
Westminster/John Knox Press and the Lutterworth Press for
permission to use the extract from *New Testament Apocrypha*, Volumes
I and II edited by Edgar Hennecke and Wilhelm Schneemelcher,
quoted on p. 22
Sister Sheila Margaret for permission to reproduce the poem
'Transfiguration', quoted on p. 89

Biblical quotations are from *The New Jerusalem Bible*,
published and copyright 1985 by Darton, Longman and Todd Ltd
and Doubleday & Co Inc. and used by permission

Phototypeset by Intype, London
Printed and bound in Great Britain
by Page Bros, Norwich

In memory of Arthur Michael Ramsey
Archbishop of Canterbury 1961–74

Contents

Foreword

Many theologians – especially in the Eastern Christian tradition – have found the gospel narratives of the Lord's Transfiguration to be a way in to reflection on the most central mysteries of the Christian faith, even the very nature of God. The stories in the first three gospels read like a sketch for the great meditations of St John on the showing of God's glory in the vulnerable humanity of Jesus.

In this book, Rob Marshall takes us into the depths of the narratives, so as to show how the Transfiguration impels us both to looking and to listening – to a deeper and deeper attention to God, that will issue in the communication to the world of the *joy* of God's presence. This book manages to combine painstaking exegesis of the actual familiar texts, bringing some very fresh insights out of them, with plenty of theology – in the classical and ancient sense of drawing us actively into the worship of God. Not the least achievement of these pages is to make *all* of us look to the reality of transfiguration as it appears in our own lives as baptised and witnessing believers.

To have our attention steered back to this story, to the terror and ecstasy of encounter with God in the flesh and blood of Jesus, is to be recalled to why there is a Church at all: not to promote ideas, not to sanction morals – though ideas and morality flow from the vision – but to witness to a compelling beauty, the radiance of a self-sharing, self-bestowing love sustaining all. Fortunately, at many times when the Church has been lured away from this conviction, there have been theologians who have firmly set our priorities before us. Even in the twentieth-century Church, weighed down with the complex burdens of ideas and moralities in dispute, such witness has been borne. Many will think of Michael Ramsey, to whose loved memory this book is dedicated. Rob Marshall has drunk from the same wells of study and prayer together, and his reflections will help many rediscover something of the heart of the Church's life and hope.

ROWAN WILLIAMS
Bishop of Monmouth

Introduction

The Transfiguration of Jesus has always had a particular poignancy and relevance for me. When I was a young Christian, coming from a non-church-going background, the first parish church I attended was dedicated to the Transfiguration. It became a source of inspiration for me. God could and did transform people's lives in the same way that he transfigured his only Son on the holy mountain.

As a priest serving in three Anglican parishes so far, I have endeavoured to reclaim locally the Transfiguration of Jesus as a major Feast Day. In Leeds and Otley where I served as a curate I frequently heard people remark, 'Oh, he's not on about the Transfiguration again!' When I was vicar of Embsay with Eastby, in the Yorkshire Dales, we made a big occasion of the Feast of the Transfiguration each year on 6th August. We would climb a nearby hill at six o'clock in the morning to thank God for that journey of Peter, James and John with Jesus. Then, after the Sung Eucharist in the evening, we had a summer social occasion. But in most churches up and down the land, the Transfiguration is sadly ignored. In fact, many people do not understand it: it remains an enigma.

The same is true in the field of biblical scholarship. Any serious student of the New Testament would agree that its relative importance within the life of Jesus is not reflected in theological books and articles. Still less does the Transfiguration feature in popular Christian writing on modern spirituality or morality. Whilst other key events and words and works of Jesus gain ample examination and discussion, the Transfiguration remains largely ignored and unappreciated.

In this book I shall attempt to redress the balance by sharing the importance of this momentous event in the life of Jesus, and examining its significance for us as individuals and as the Church. It is not an academic work, although I have drawn on biblical scholarship. My aim throughout has been to approach the Transfiguration in an accessible way and to open up doors of understanding and insight.

The issues affecting the lives of the first Christians reveal a great deal to us of their understanding of Jesus. Whilst Mark's account of the Transfiguration (9:2–8) is almost certainly the first and, therefore, the most important, I believe that some older Transfiguration traditions, which can be associated with the apostle Peter, have been placed in the context of 2 Peter. We need to understand the 2 Peter account before proceeding to that of Mark. The additions of Matthew and Luke can then be fully appreciated.

There is a separate chapter on each of the Gospel writers in which I analyse their own understanding of the Transfiguration. Mark sets the context of the story in the Gospels after Caesarea Philippi and stresses the importance of discipleship. Matthew sees Jesus as a great Old Testament figure who is fulfilling what was expected of him as the Messiah. Luke brings in the theme of glory, prayer and suffering in his own unique way. Only after assessing the biblical sources and evidence can we look at what the critics have made of the Transfiguration of Jesus. Then we can move on to assess how it can help us in our own lives, worship and pilgrimage today.

I am indebted to the former Archbishop of Canterbury, Bishop Michael Ramsey, for more than five years of friendship before his death in April 1988. The Transfiguration was a source of endless fascination for him and his influence on me throughout the book is obvious; he was the first to urge me to write it. I would also like to thank the parishes in which I have served, the many pilgrim groups who have journeyed with me to the top of Mount Tabor, and my own family and friends for their support and encouragement.

ROB MARSHALL
London, 1994

1. Beauty on the Mountain

After this our Lord showed himself, in glory even greater than I had ever seen before. (Julian of Norwich)

In many ways the Transfiguration of Jesus acts as a major turning point in the Gospels of Mark, Matthew and Luke. Attempts throughout the centuries to come up with a satisfactory theological explanation of the story have failed. It does not fit into any of the accepted categories, such as 'miracle' or 'parable'. It is the story's unique character which makes it difficult to understand: 'the story of the Transfiguration is without parallel in the gospels, a fact which makes its interpretation all the more problematic.'[1]

At a time when spiritual matters are once again becoming increasingly important to people, the Transfiguration of Jesus is undiscovered treasure. We live in a world where individuals, and society as a whole, live for the moment. Ours is a community in which materialism – possessions – counts for a lot. But it is also a world in which death intervenes and makes a nonsense out of short-term gain and ideology. People are waking up to the issue of spirituality and for the Christian Church this is a time of great challenge and evangelism. In this context the events which took place on a high and lonely mountain towards the end of Jesus' Galilean ministry need to be understood by individuals and the Church as a whole. We need to rediscover the fascination which the Transfiguration had for the first believers.

1

Biblical background

The symbolism of the story is enormously exciting. After months of preaching the coming of the Kingdom of God, Jesus ascends the mountain and a glorious event takes place. Shortly after Peter has confessed him as Messiah at Caesarea Philippi (Mark 8), Jesus is transfigured before his three chosen disciples, Peter, James and John. Moses and Elijah witness all that follows. The disciples experience the glory of the Lord embodied in the person of Jesus. God confirms that Jesus is the Son of God when a voice, similar to that at Jesus' baptism, is heard speaking through a cloud.

The Transfiguration of Jesus is recorded in all three Synoptic Gospels (Mark 9:2–8; Matthew 17:1–8, Luke 9:28–36). Each account is basically the same but each writer also adds his own individual detail and characteristics. I will look at each of these stories individually in order to assess the impact of the Gospel evidence as a whole. St John omits the Transfiguration from his Gospel altogether because it does not fit into his overall scheme. He is more concerned with the gradual revelation of God's glory throughout his Gospel rather than in one dramatic moment. The following verse (John 1:14) explains how this gradual revelation will take place: 'The word became flesh, he lived among us, and we saw his glory, the glory that he has from the Father as only Son of the Father, full of grace and truth.'

The author of 2 Peter also claims to be an eyewitness to the event and provides us with an outline of the story. The debate about the origin and authorship of this Epistle has centred on whether authentic material directly from the apostle Peter was used in the composition of a document which Peter almost certainly did not write. The Transfiguration could hold a key here. There is also a reference to the Transfiguration in the Apocalypse of Peter which I will refer to again in the next chapter. St Paul uses the Greek verb 'to transfigure' on one occasion: 'And all of us, with our unveiled faces like mirrors reflecting the glory of the Lord are being transformed into the image that we reflect in brighter and brighter glory; this is the working of the Lord who is the Spirit.' (2 Corinthians 3:18). I will examine this verse too in a later chapter.

Slow development

In the life of the Church, however, the Transfiguration of Jesus remains largely ignored. It has always been on the fringe rather than in the centre of the Church's theology, liturgy and spirituality. The Early Church recognised its importance but it was some time before it was commemorated as a major Feast Day in the Church's life. Unlike other key events such as the Visitation, the Annunciation, the Resurrection and the Ascension, the Transfiguration curiously remains an enigma. Whilst other events may beg questions of faith and understanding, most churchgoers are unaware of the Transfiguration story or its significance. In the worshipping life of the Orthodox Church it has figured more prominently then in the West. In the Eastern Church the Feast dates back to about the fourth century when the first church was dedicated on the summit of Mount Tabor.

In the writings of the Eastern Church Fathers the Transfiguration is used to highlight the harmony between the Old and New Testaments. Irenaeus points out that neither Moses nor Elijah was able to see the face of God during his lifetime (1 Kings 19:12; Exodus 33:20–33), but on the mountain of the Transfiguration the glory of God is revealed to them both. Tertullian makes several references to the unity of the revelation contained in both the Old and New Testaments and believes the Transfiguration to be confirmation that the fullness of the revelation resides in the person of Christ. Origen, meanwhile, believed that the Transfiguration was a challenge to the spirituality of all believers. It was an event of great encouragement to those on earth as they journeyed towards the eternal glory which would be revealed in eternity. The mystery revealed on Mount Tabor is for everyone.

Gregory of Nazianzen is intrigued by the similarity

3

between Moses on Mount Sinai and Peter on Mount Tabor. It was on the holy mountain of the Transfiguration that Peter experienced the reality of God's glory which would fill the Church. In the period between the fifth century and the fourteenth century the Transfiguration figured in many of the writings of the Eastern Fathers. Orthodox theologians today believe that the Transfiguration is one of only two moments in Christ's life when the glory of God is made visible for all to see. As Timothy Ware explains, the two moments are: 'the Transfiguration, when on Mount Tabor the uncreated light of His Godhead shone visibly through the garments of his flesh; and the Resurrection, when the tomb burst open under the pressure of divine life, and Christ returned triumphant from the dead.'[2]

In the East the emphasis was always on the spiritual dimensions that the Transfiguration revealed to all believers. In Western Christianity there has been a much greater stress on the impact of the Transfiguration on the disciples. Thus the Latin Fathers tended to concentrate on the ethical and historical dimensions which the Transfiguration introduced into the Christian faith. The glory of Jesus is revealed to Peter, James and John and there is a promise that this will also be shared by all believers in the future. St Augustine makes a passing reference to the Transfiguration, pointing out that the light which illumines every person had come into the world and that Jesus offers to all of us the transformation of our souls. The Transfiguration was not accepted officially by Rome until the fifteenth century, when Callistus III suggested it as an appropriate Feast Day to celebrate the victory over the Turks in Belgrade on 6 August 1456.

The traditional Feast Day of the Transfiguration remains 6th August. The first evidence of this date in the Western Church goes back to the ninth century and is found in Spain. The Crusaders witnessed the memorial of this great Feast on Mount Tabor and brought news of it home. It was adopted by the religious community at Cluny in France, from where it spread to various Christian communities. The Transfiguration has been celebrated on 6 August ever since; but a basic ignorance of it in the West has been and remains

4

very real. As August is in the main holiday period the festival is often overlooked. School children have broken up for the summer and most churches are in holiday mode. Any celebration tends to be 'low key'.

The Roman Catholic Church has attempted to include the Transfiguration in its Lectionary on other important days during the year as well as 6 August. The Church in England designated its regular observance in 1487 when the Convocation of Canterbury decreed that it should be celebrated throughout the country. But the Church of England's first English Prayer Book, published in 1549, completely ignored the Feast on the grounds that it was not sufficiently important or central to Our Lord's life. Only in 1561 was it restored as a 'black letter' day, listed in the calendar but without its own Collect, Epistle and Gospel. The American and Scottish churches both gave the Transfiguration 'full status' before the Church of England did so. The first time that a Prayer Book of the Church of England printed a Collect, Epistle and Gospel of the Transfiguration was in the 1928 Prayer Book revision. This may explain something of the general lack of interest and understanding surrounding the Transfiguration of Jesus amongst Christians and theologians in Britain. *The Alternative Service Book* (ASB, 1980) continues the tradition of the 1928 revision by providing us with readings for the Feast Day (Exodus 34: 29–end; 2 Corinthians 3:4–end; Luke 9:28–36) and the following Collect:

> Almighty Father,
> whose Son was revealed in majesty
> before he suffered death upon the cross:
> give us faith to perceive his glory,
> that we may be strengthened to suffer with him
> and be changed into his likeness, from glory to glory;
> who is alive and reigns with you and the Holy Spirit,
> one God, now and for ever. Amen

The Transfiguration story is also the Gospel reading on the fourth Sunday in Lent in the ASB. This, however, always

5

clashes with Mothering Sunday and many parishes again ignore the Transfiguration. In other denominations it is often overlooked altogether.

To most Christians today the Transfiguration is a mystery. It is a story they have largely missed out on. Ask any congregation, during the course of a sermon, what happened on the mountain of the Transfiguration and few would have any idea. It is not a story that Sunday School teachers find easy to teach. Adult Education or Bible Study Groups also struggle with the Transfiguration. Somehow, over the centuries, it has remained largely untouched by ordinary Christians who feel that it is too complicated or difficult to understand. This applies also to preachers and theologians who are easily sidetracked into a sermon about divine revelation, the glory of Moses and Elijah, the need to listen, rather than the overall importance of this momentous event in the life of Christ.

It is also worth noting that the Transfiguration of Jesus is not mentioned in either the Nicean or the Apostle's Creed. It has no obvious place in any mainstream liturgy of the Churches. There are few well-known hymns about the Transfiguration. Perhaps the best known is ''Tis Good Lord To Be Here' written by J. A. Robinson but even this is sung very rarely:

> 'Tis good, Lord, to be here!
> Thy glory fills the night;
> Thy face and garments, like the sun,
> Shine with unborrowed light.

> 'Tis good, Lord, to be here,
> Thy beauty to behold,
> Where Moses and Elijah stand,
> Thy messengers of old.

> Fulfiller of the past!
> Promise of things to be!
> We hail thy body glorified,
> And our redemption see.

Before we taste of death,
We see thy Kingdom come;
We fain would hold the vision bright,
And make this hill our home.

'Tis good, Lord, to be here!
Yet we may not remain;
But since thou bidst us leave the mount
Come with us to the plain.

There are few well-known prayers which are synonymous
with the event. Even the number of serious books written
on the subject is minimal. It is not a theme that has moved
many great artists, poets or musicians, though there are
some notable exceptions. For instance, there is a marvellous
painting by Raphael hanging in St Peter's Bascilica in Rome.
It shows a radiant Christ surrounded by white light; Moses
and Elijah look on whilst the three disciples are also in
awe of their transfigured Lord. More recently, the theme of
transfiguration inspired Kevin Mills, who wrote this poem
entitled 'Transfiguration':

Days all sun-steeped and glorious,
hot with bright flowers
and sweet with fellowship's fruit,
mingle with
days all dark-drenched and aching,
cold without mornings,
and sour with grapes of solitude
in memory's tide.

The sour sweet river
sprays into the air
soft light in particles
in an aura of pale yellow time,
suspended around my past,
bringing about a
transfiguration
of my days.

> The charcoal spars
> of the burnt bridge of summer
> crumble on to the paper-white foam
> in powder-black sketches
> of people and places –
> a season depicted with nothing but shadows,
> cast in the warm glance
> of memory's sun.

At a recent exhibition of Russian icons at the Victoria and Albert Museum in London (1993) there were several examples of how the Transfiguration influenced various artists. The explanation near to an icon cloth from Moscow read: 'During the second half of the fourteenth century Byzantine intellectual and spiritual life concentrated on the Transfiguration as an event and as an image. It was held that the blinding light witnessed on Mount Tabor was not a natural or created phenomenon. It was the "uncreated" light of divine energy which belongs to the eternal nature of God.' One of my favourite icons of the Transfiguration dates back to the fifteenth century and the school of Novogorod. The whole scene is depicted within a large circle which expands as it becomes progressively lighter. The entire scene is in complete sunlight with no shadows.

Some writers have suggested that the Transfiguration has its significance outside the realms of the ordinary and, therefore, it feels odd in the Gospel sequence: 'This pericope (story) is unique in form, character and position. Like the baptism story it is a "myth" in depicting the activity of the supernatural in physical terms.'[3] The story has therefore continued to baffle Bible readers, worshippers, theologians and artists over the years.

In this book I will attempt to delve into this mystery. My aim is to explain why the Transfiguration is crucial to our overall understanding of the person of Jesus. I firmly believe that it can help us in a real and liberating way as we live out Christian lives in our own time and generation. Certainly, it is a story which has presented itself to me in a variety of ways. Four key events are in mind as I think about the influence of the Transfiguration story on me as a youngster in the North of England, as a theological student and now as a priest.

The parish church of North Newington, Kingston upon Hull, was demolished in 1974 after architects found that it had suspect foundations. It was one of the few Church of England parish churches dedicated to the Transfiguration. By happy coincidence, the Church of the Transfiguration was my own parish church as a child. I vividly remember the beautiful stained-glass windows above the altar depicting events on the holy mountain. When the church was demolished the Transfiguration windows were removed to the Roman Catholic Church of the Holy Name near Cottingham. Those windows tell the story of the Transfiguration in a vivid and memorable way: Jesus, in the centre, radiated the glory of God; Moses and Elijah took pride of place on either side; Peter, James and John were at the feet of these central figures. I remember spending a good deal of time looking at these windows, especially when the sun's rays made them appear even brighter. Above the head of Jesus was a cloud from which a voice was speaking the words inscribed underneath the window: 'This is my beloved son; listen to him.' The challenge embodied in those words was a deep one and, for many years, those windows *were* the Transfiguration. They seemed to explain and unravel the mystery for me as a child.

My interest in the story deepened further when I was a second-year student in the Department of Biblical Studies at Sheffield University. I was asked to select a New Testament subject on which I would have to write a dissertation. I had no doubts about which subject I would like to tackle. But my tutor, Dr Bruce Chilton, was rather surprised when I told him that I would like to study the Transfiguration. I remember him commenting during our interview: 'There is very little written, particularly in English; you may struggle, but have a go!' It was during that year that I realised for the first time how far the story of the Transfiguration is ignored in much New Testament theological study. Of course, all the Gospel commentaries have sections on the story as it appears in the relevant Gospels. But there is hardly anything of note written on the story and its implications. The shelves of many theological libraries are stacked with journals and books on a wide range of great theological subjects – the incarnation, the miracles, parables and temptation, the resurrection, the ascension and Pauline theology – but the Transfiguration remains ignored and largely unappreciated. I was fascinated by the paucity of references to the Transfiguration in serious theological study, which made my thesis all the more difficult!

But there was one notable exception. Michael Ramsey was the 100th Archbishop of Canterbury; during 1961–74 he served as head of the Anglican Communion. He was to be the next major influence on me as I moved from Sheffield to Durham in 1981. I decided to study the Transfiguration further in the Department of Theology there and Dr Andrew Chesters, my tutor, suggested that someone not far away might well be of use to me. Bishop Ramsey lived in retirement with his wife, Joan, no more than forty yards from my own front door. I wrote to him and he responded promptly. He was delighted that I was studying the Transfiguration of Jesus and invited me to breakfast. That 'Transfiguration Breakfast' with Bishop Ramsey was a revelation. He was a fount of wisdom, with specific views on the subject and he was the last scholar to write an authoritative book on it in this country.[4]

His enthusiasm for the story was infectious: 'The radiance is a vision of Jesus as he would be when he returns in glory. The comment of St Basil is true to the meaning: Peter and the sons of thunder saw his beauty on the mountain, outshining the brightness of the sun, and they were deemed worthy to receive the anticipation of his glorious parousia with their eyes. Jesus is seen in glory in spite of the coming suffering and death. One day it would be known that the glory is not in spite of the suffering and death, but in its very midst. But that day had not yet come.'[5] He was the first person to suggest that I should write this book.

Stained-glass windows, university studies and an Archbishop of Canterbury all added excitement and joy to my discovery of the Transfiguration as a story of great mystery and depth. But there was another, very significant, event which finally inspired me to write a book about this episode in Jesus' life. My first visit to the Holy Land in 1988 provided another Transfiguration experience. I was one of more than thirty pilgrims on a tour bus. Our guide, Leon Segal, pointed out a lonely mountain as we were journeying from Tel Aviv to the Galilee region early one morning: 'If you look to the right you will see a mountain; a high mountain. And on top you can see a church; it looks very tiny from here, but this is the Church of the Transfiguration.' I could hardly believe my eyes. As I looked at the mountain, more than fifteen years of pondering and reflection, questions and prayers, focused on that one place. Tabor is 588 metres high and is known locally in Arabic as 'The Bull Mountain'. In the Jewish War of 66 AD it was a natural defence for Galilee in front-line battles with the Romans. In 1799 Napoleon defeated the Turks here.

Perhaps this was not exactly the place. Michael Ramsey frequently argued that Mount Hermon was an equally good candidate – more remote and much higher. The debate about which mountain was historically the site of the Transfiguration goes on, but the fact remains that Mount Tabor is a designated place of Christian worship and pilgrimage to the Transfiguration. The village of Dabburiya squats about one-third of the way up the mountain and the road ends there. So you leave your pilgrim coach and take special taxis, driven by local Bedouin drivers, up the hairpin road to the top, though it is also possible to walk there and back within a day.

The top of the mountain is divided between the Greek Orthodox and Franciscan communities and there is a wall separating the two. The Roman Catholic Church has a guest house along with a small gift shop. Once you leave your taxi at the top of the mountain there is an immediate feeling of peace and tranquility. The Church of the Transfiguration is quite beautiful. The open crypt preserves what remains of the Crusader apse. The mosaics around the building serve as reminders to pilgrims of the birth, the last supper, the death and resurrection of Jesus and there are two chapels (dedicated to Moses and Elijah) at the back of the church. I now take pilgrim groups there every year and make a habit of ending each tour at the top of the mountain, looking south to Jerusalem and north to the Sea of Galilee. Regular visits to the Transfiguration site have further stimulated my basic conviction that we need to attach greater emphasis to this glorious event and to take it much more seriously.

'The story of the Transfiguration of Jesus on the mountain has had its impact upon Christian spirituality through the centuries. It is a story of symbols – the Light, the Witnesses, the cloud and the Voice – symbols which speak to us still.'[6] In a memorial service to Michael Ramsey at York Minster a few months after his death, John Habgood, the Archbishop of York, stressed the importance of the Transfiguration in the life and ministry of the former Archbishop of Canterbury: 'The Transfiguration sums up much of what the Gospel is all about. It is a mirror in which the Christian mystery is seen in its unity. The transfiguration of suffering, the transfiguration of knowledge, the transfiguration of the world.' Before exploring those symbols in more detail, I will look first at the biblical evidence.

2. Biblical Pointers

The three Synoptic writers place this narrative in the same place, following Peter's confession, the first announcement of the Passion, and the words of Jesus on the suffering of the disciples and the future glory of the Son of Man. The Transfiguration continues these themes: glory, Sonship and the necessity of Christ's suffering. (David Hill)[1]

The Transfiguration contains a whole series of biblical images and ideas that help us to understand the person of Jesus in a proper context. The New Testament imagery is heavily dependent on the Old Testament. There are four accounts of the Transfiguration in the New Testament – three in the Gospels and another in the Letters of the Early Church. Mark, Matthew and Luke write about events on the mountaintop and the other account is in the Second Epistle of St Peter. The three evangelists all record the story at roughly the same chronological point in the ministry of Jesus: after much teaching about the Kingdom of God in and around the Galilee region, Peter confesses Jesus as the Messiah at Caesarea Phillippi. Kirk, writing in 1931, observed: 'Before the earliest gospel had assumed its present shape, the church had fixed upon the Transfiguration as the central moment of the Lord's earthly life.'[2] The account in 2 Peter 1:16–19 is a relatively ignored version of the Transfiguration story and, as we shall see, it is extremely important.

Each of the three evangelists has an individual approach to the Transfiguration story but there is also a great deal

13

which they have in common. The following details are mentioned in all three Gospel accounts:

- the event takes place about a week after an unspecified occasion;
- Peter, James and John accompany Jesus;
- the place is a high mountain;
- Jesus' appearance changes dramatically;
- Elijah and Moses appear with Jesus;
- Peter speaks out and makes reference to building tabernacles;
- a cloud appears and a voice speaks from it.

Each Gospel writer creates his own story out of these central themes. I shall look more closely at the individual characteristics of each evangelist in the next few chapters.

First, I will examine the sources and that critical period between the actual historical event and the subsequent recording of it in written form. Whilst I firmly believe that an historical event of extraordinary significance did take place on the mountain, it is impossible for us to know exactly what happened, and when and how. Not all scholars agree that the Transfiguration actually happened. As I shall show in discussion throughout this book, there are many who regard the Transfiguration purely as a visionary experience of the disciples. Because the story has sometimes been misunderstood, some people have suggested that the event may be a creation of the evangelists to confirm Jesus' Messiahship. A period of 'story telling' from one individual or community to another was how many of the words and works of Jesus were preserved. This oral tradition meant that what Jesus said and did was passed on by word of mouth for many years after his resurrection and obviously helped shape the sources which influenced the evangelists. As the story of the Transfiguration of Jesus was told and retold, different emphases and interpretations were added.

14

Mark as the first Gospel

The Transfiguration in Mark is the most important account in the New Testament. Theologians have traditionally identified Mark as the John Mark mentioned in the Acts of the Apostles (12:12, 25; 13:5, 13; 15:37) and in some of the Epistles (2 Timothy 4:11; 1 Peter 5:13). His mother was called Mary (Acts 12:12) and was a member of the Jerusalem Church. John Mark seems to have had a close association with both Peter (which I will explore in a moment) and Paul. Most scholars would agree that the Gospel of Mark dates from the period AD 66–70; this would suggest that the Gospel was finally written down after the death of St Peter. Mark was the first of the four Gospels to be written down. St Augustine believed that Mark had copied and abbreviated Matthew's Gospel and this view was widely accepted until the nineteenth century when it began to be challenged. As Hooker says: 'Nineteenth century New Testament scholarship was dominated by the quest for the historical Jesus – the desire to discover Jesus as he really was, not as the church had interpreted him – and in that quest Mark took on a new importance.'[3]

Peter the eyewitness

Peter was one of the three disciples present with Jesus on the mountain of the Transfiguration, and his role in the development of the story within the Early Church is fascinating.

Most commentators agree that St Peter had a close working relationship with St Mark and played a key role in the formation of the Gospel of Mark. Papias, in a famous quote, suggests that Peter was Mark's interpreter[4] and theologians have argued about the meaning of this crucial word. Peter was Jesus' closest disciple and was present at many key moments in Our Lord's life. It is certain that Mark himself was not present at the same events. Thus Mark interpreted, in written form, the events that Peter had seen, recounted, remembered and experienced; this would include Peter's reminiscences, in Aramaic, of the life and ministry of Jesus, written down by Mark in Greek. There is much material in the Gospel of Mark which is the work of an eyewitness. Ralph Martin believes that this data could not have been Mark's work without someone like Peter to assist him.[5] Peter's prominence suggests that he is the source of much material throughout the Gospel (for example, 3:5, 7:34, 9:36). In his commentary on Mark's Gospel, Cranfield is certain that 'Peter is likely to have remembered not only particular incidents but also the general course of the ministry of Jesus'.[6]

Only those present on the mountain could have known who was there, what was said and the drama of the occasion. The direct quote from the mouth of St Peter in the Transfiguration story adds weight to the view that Peter is Mark's main source. Peter plays a prominent role throughout the whole Gospel and is part of the inner group of three disciples who are present with Jesus at key times. It would seem reasonable to conclude that Mark, as Peter's interpreter, passed on details and information about what happened on the mountain of the Transfiguration. Mark then built on these as he wrote down his Transfiguration story. In other words, Mark brought to life, in a coherent way, the life and ministry of Jesus as Peter remembered it. He interpreted for Peter in written form what the Apostle had been preaching and teaching throughout the region in which he travelled. And as Mark was the first to compose his Gospel, both the Matthean and Lucan accounts borrow heavily from Mark.

It is clear that both Matthew and Luke used additional sources and material, though I shall not examine these in great detail here. It is agreed, for instance, that both had sources which were exclusive to them – commonly known as M (Matthew) and L (Luke). The reference to Jesus praying, the talk about the exodus and the use of the word *doxa* could well belong to the L source. What is important for us is the conclusion that Mark wrote first and that he acted as Peter's interpreter. St Peter was widely respected throughout the Early Church and he was committed to growth and renewal based on the words and works of Jesus.

16

Clues from 2 Peter

The account in this Epistle is the most under-estimated and ignored, yet it is very significant as we consider Peter's role in the transmission of the story. Just as it is now generally believed that Mark was the first Gospel, so it is also postulated that, although 1 Peter was probably written by Peter, the Second Letter almost certainly was not. The background to 2 Peter is a mystery to scholars. Questions of authorship, date, intention and origin remain unresolved. It was accepted into the Canon only in the fourth century and with greater hesitation than for any other New Testament document. No book in the Canon is quoted less frequently in the writings of the Fathers. Origen, perhaps, explains this in writing: 'Peter left one acknowledged Epistle and perhaps a second; for this is contested.' Eusebius accepts that 2 Peter was a disputed work but insists that many regard it as genuine, even though he had grave doubts himself.[7] At the time of the Reformation, Luther was happy to accept 2 Peter as authentic, whilst Erasmus rejected it. Calvin was uncertain. More generally, in our own day, opinion seems to have hardened against the authenticity of the Epistle, though Michael Green has suggested that we need to look at the Epistle again because it contains some important material.[8]

Readers of 1 and 2 Peter are quick to notice different styles and content. This suggests that they were certainly written by different people. The Greek of the First Epistle is smooth and intellectually composed, with free-flowing participles and a definite coherence of thought. In contrast, the style of the Second is more highly coloured, effusive and pompous; the words are often bookish and artificial. Green argues that this may simply be as a result of a change of scribe but the overall view is that we are, in fact dealing with two different authors. The date is also a problem. The majority of scholars believe that the Epistle was written down some time between 100–110 AD. Peter would have been dead for about forty years – a fact almost confirmed by a reference in 2 Peter 3:4: ' "What has happened to the promise of his coming?" they will say, "Since our Fathers died everything has gone on just as it has since the beginning of creation." '

The first generation of Christians, who had expected Jesus' immediate return, had already died. Kelly believes that the author of 2 Peter relies heavily on material from Jude which is also dated much later.[9] A close examination of the two Epistles underlines the point. The fact that St Peter is unlikely to have been the author of the Second Epistle and that it may well have been composed some forty years after his death suggests that the Transfiguration story in 2 Peter 1 could easily be dismissed as a summary of what is contained in Matthew, Mark and Luke. But closer examination of the text of the Epistle reveals an association with reminiscences, events and sayings that some would call 'apostolic testimony'. The Transfiguration is one such story where the author suggests that they were 'eyewitnesses of his majesty'. The other passages include the prophecy of Peter's own death (1:14), the denial of the Lord Jesus by Peter (2:1) and that this is indeed the second letter of, at least, two (3:1). Such references suggest that despite a later date and different grammatical style there would seem to be a certain reliance on material which many in the Early Church viewed as 'Peter material'.

The most popular suggestion is that someone assumed the identity of St Peter and used material which was undoubtedly associated with him. As early as 1921, Harrison said that in assuming the guise of Peter the author of 2 Peter 'was not conscious of misrepresenting the apostle in any way; he was not consciously deceiving anybody; it is not indeed necessary to suppose that he did deceive anybody.'[10] From this it is concluded that 2 Peter was not written by St Peter but that the author used authentic 'Peter material' in an attempt to add credibility and authority to his Epistle. The Transfiguration of Jesus is one such story and, despite its context here, may well tell us something about the kind of source which Mark also used if we directly identify it as 'Peter material'.

With regard to the story of the Transfiguration of Jesus in 2 Peter, it contains the following interesting elements:

- the apostles see the majesty of God in Jesus;
- the glory of God is repeatedly referred to;
- the words spoken by the voice of God are very similar to those of the voice in the Gospel stories;
- it takes place on a mountain.

2 Peter 1:16–18

(16) When we told you about the power and the coming of our Lord Jesus Christ, we were not slavishly repeating cleverly invented myths; no, we had seen his majesty with our own eyes. (17) He was honoured and glorified by God the Father, when a voice came to him from the transcendent Glory, This is my Son, the Beloved; he enjoys my favour. (18) We ourselves heard this voice from heaven, when we were with him on the holy mountain.

The main gist of the Transfiguration story in the Epistle is the same as in the synoptics. There is, however, much less detail. The story is simpler with less drama, but the prominence of the divine voice, the sharing of the glory between God and Christ and the suggestion that the eyewitness was, in fact, present all add weight to the possibility that here we have the nub of what Peter told Mark. This could well be 'Peter material' of the Transfiguration used by a later author to give credence to the view that Peter himself was, in fact, the author of 2 Peter. Mark may have had access to additional material or another source which would explain why his account is richer in detail. Let us look at this version of events more closely.

v. 16 When we told you about the power and the coming of our Lord Jesus Christ, we were not slavishly repeating cleverly invented myths; no, we had seen his majesty with our own eyes.

This verse is very powerful apostolic witness to the power and majesty of Jesus. Those present see his power and coming on the mountaintop with their own eyes. They were not repeating cleverly invented myths. There has been great debate as to whom the 'we' refers to but many accept the suggestion that Peter, James and John were the apostles concerned and that this refers to them. It might also include Moses and Elijah. This 'inner group' or cabinet of disciples

19

would have been accepted by the Early Church. The power and majesty of Jesus were not a 'cleverly invented myth' or a 'tale artfully spun' (NEB) against false teachers. Christianity was under attack from various religious groups. What had Jesus achieved? By what authority did these Christians continue? There were also internal disagreements within the Christian community about many practical issues. One such debate was over when the second coming of Jesus would take place. Doubts were being expressed as to whether or not it would ever take place; the author of 2 Peter writes against such doubt and believes that it will take place in the fullness of time.

His use of the words *dunamis* (power) and *parousia* (might/coming) adds theological weight to this verse. The power of Jesus is temporarily revealed on the Transfiguration mountain and is seen again at the resurrection. This underlines the Orthodox understanding which I explained in the last chapter. *Parousia* can mean 'presence', 'coming' or 'might' but, with 2 Peter 3:4ff. very much in mind, it seems that the author is concerned with the power and presence of Jesus *now* as he awaits his return. Both words – power and coming – are best understood in the light of Jesus' expected return in glory. The disciples have already witnessed both on the Transfiguration mountain. The suffering of Jesus, his resurrection and ascension, can be understood only in the context of Jesus' future return; when the glory and power and presence of Jesus is made perfect. I will look more closely at the connection between Transfiguration and the Second Coming of Jesus in a later chapter.

v. 17 He was honoured and glorified by God the Father, when a voice came to him from the transcendent Glory, This is my Son, the beloved; he enjoys my favour.

God is revealed as the instigator of the glorious scene. The voice of God is introduced and Jesus is affirmed as the Son of God. The verse is packed with detail. Robson wrote in 1945 that this verse is 'the sign manual of one who knows' exactly what took place on the holy mountain.[11] Jesus is said to have received *time* (honour) and *doxa* (glory). The Greek word *time* is not uncommon (cf. Hebrews 2:7; 3:3; Revelation 5:12) and usually describes the victory of Jesus over death and evil. Honour and glory are given to Our Lord from 'the Father'. None of the Gospel accounts actually makes it clear that it is God speaking but this is taken for granted. Parallels with the baptism story of Jesus will be explored later.

It is interesting to note that the Greek verb *metamorphe* (transfigured) does not appear. 'Glory' and 'honour' describe the transfigured state of Christ (as in Luke) and the verb 'to be transfigured' is later introduced by Mark and Matthew. The 'honour' and 'glory' here are signs to those present that Jesus possesses an honour and a glory which are temporarily revealed at the Transfiguration but which will be revealed more fully at the *parousia*. This is the thrust of Boobyer's theory which I will explore later. The words spoken by the voice are very similar to those in Matthew 17:6. The presence of these words adds weight to the notion that it is 'Peter material' which is being used here.

v. 18 We ourselves heard this voice from heaven, when we were with him on the holy mountain.

Once again it is clear that we are dealing with eyewitness material. This verse confirms that events on the holy mountain had a profound effect on those present. It is a reminiscence, a reflection on the significance of a major event in the life of Jesus. If Mark had this source or story at his fingertips it is easy to see how he wove it into the context of his Gospel. This Epistle contains the most vivid reference to the Transfiguration of Jesus outside the Gospels. The author was probably not St Peter but he did use material which was closely associated with the apostle. Much of the Letter is a defence of the delay in the Second Coming which many expected earlier. The Transfiguration is a story of power, glory, might and presence. Jesus, the Son of God, has already defeated suffering and death and will reveal his glory in the future when he finally returns in splendour. Understood correctly in 2 Peter, the Transfiguration is a revelation given beforehand of what Jesus will be like at the Second Coming.

The Apocalypse of Peter

There is another reference to the Transfiguration in the Apocalypse of Peter – an early Christian document not included in the New Testament Canon. Two fragments of the original document are available to us – a Greek text which is known as the Akhim Fragment and an Ethiopic version which is usually attributed to Clement of Rome. Many scholars believe that the Apocalypse of Peter existed on its own within the Early Church as a separate document. The Akhim Fragment contains a narrative of the Transfiguration of Jesus which bears some similarity to the synoptic accounts but it is the Ethiopic version of the Apocalypse which is more important to us. Here is a translation provided for us by Hennecke in his *New Testament Apocrypha*:[12]

> And my Lord Jesus Christ, our King, said to me: 'Let us go into the holy mountain.' And his disciples went with him praying. And behold there were two men, and we could not look on their faces, for a light came from them which shone more than the sun and their raiment was also glistening and cannot be described, and there is no thing sufficient to be compared to them in this world.
>
> And its gentleness ... that no mouth is able to express the beauty of their form. For their aspect was astonishing and wonderful. And the other, great, I say, shines in his appearance more than hail (crystal). Flowers of roses is the likeness of the colour of his appearance and his body ... his head. And upon his shoulders and on their foreheads was a crown of nard, a work woven from beautiful flowers; like the rainbow in water was his hair. This was the comeliness of his countenance, and he was adorned with all kinds of ornament. And when we suddenly saw them, we marvelled. And I approached God Jesus Christ and said to him, 'My Lord who is this?' And he said to me, 'These are Moses and Elias.' And I said to him, 'Where are Abram, Isaac, Jacob and the other righteous Fathers?' And my Lord and God Jesus Christ said to me, 'Have you seen the companies of the fathers; As is their rest, so also is the honour and glory of those who will be persecuted for my righteousness' sake.'

The Apocalypse of Peter is chiefly concerned with the Second Coming of Jesus. The venue is the Mount of Olives; this is the same as in Mark 13:3 where a conversation about the Second Coming also takes place on the Mount of Olives. In the verses immediately before the above extract the circumstances in which the Second Coming will take place are being discussed. This reinforces the view that, as in 2 Peter, those in the Early Church always connected the Transfiguration with the Second Coming of Jesus. The glory of the transfigured Lord is similar to that which Jesus will have when he returns as the Son of Man. Moses and Elijah share in that glory. The Christological link between the Transfiguration and the *parousia* is the glory of God. The Transfiguration in the Apocalypse of Peter is present proof of future events.

The Transfiguration and the Early Church

So what does the account in 2 Peter and this reference in the Apocalypse of Peter teach us about the Transfiguration? So far we have suggested that Mark, as Peter's interpreter, wrote his Gospel first and that 'Peter material' may have been used by the author of 2 Peter. This source in 2 Peter might reveal to us something of what Peter actually told Mark and that would enable us to see how Mark has edited Peter's source and what other material has been used in the context of his Gospel. The Transfiguration was one of many stories about Jesus that would have been circulating in the Early Church. Some idea of what people were thinking, understanding and expecting around this time is crucial to our understanding of the Transfiguration of Jesus. There were many issues being debated in the Early Church, including authority, leadership, doctrine, relationships, stewardship and loyalty to Christ in the face of persecution. Boobyer is right to suggest that the Epistles show many of the internal issues facing the Church, whilst the formation of the Gospels was also affected by the Early Church's understanding of who Jesus was. St Paul, for example, describes himself as the bearer of divine revelation (Romans 15:18; 2 Corinthians

23

13:3) which is grounded in the knowledge that Jesus has been raised from the dead (1 Corinthians 9:1; 15:8).

The Transfiguration story, in its concern with the revelation of divine authority and glory in the person of Jesus, would have appealed to the early Christian community. The whole thrust of the 2 Peter account is based on the understanding of historical revelation. Boobyer is certain that the story of the Transfiguration in 2 Peter is used to underline the notion that Jesus' Second Coming is imminent. But for whatever reason the author of the Epistle chose to use the Transfiguration story here, I believe that it was almost certainly an original Peter source. Mark would have been told something very similar to this and then added his own detail. The context of the Transfiguration in 2 Peter shows how the Early Church was concerned with the implications of the divine revelation of Jesus.

3. Discipleship in Action: the Gospel of Mark

In order to penetrate into the heart of those awe-inspiring mysteries with the disciples whom our Lord chose, let us listen to the holy voice of God which summons us from on high, from the mountain top. (Anastasius of Sinai, *A Sermon on the Feast of the Transfiguration*)

We cannot be certain who exactly Mark was. The Roman name Marcus was very popular and the references to Mark in the New Testament do not all apply to the same person. No one with that name is known to have been particularly close to Jesus during his ministry. John Mark who is mentioned in the Acts of Apostles was the son of Mary. He played a key role in the early days of the Jerusalem Church and his house was used for prayer (Acts 12: 12, 25). Paul and Barnabas chose him as a companion on their first missionary journey but he quarrelled with Paul and left them after a short time (Acts 13:13). Later he went on a tour of Cyprus (Acts 15:36–40) with Barnabas. The Mark mentioned in the Epistles of St Paul was a cousin of Barnabas (Colossians 4:10) and it is obvious that Paul liked him (Colossians 4:11; Philemon 24;2 Timothy 4:11). This might suggest that there had been a reconciliation between Paul and Mark if this was indeed the same person. Whilst it is not impossible that John Mark was the author we cannot be certain. Christian tradition is content with the name Mark – someone who took upon himself the task of writing the Gospel concerning Jesus Christ and who was closely associated with many sources and people surrounding the person of Jesus. Mark seemed well acquainted with St Peter.

According to Papias and Irenaeus, Mark wrote shortly after Peter's death, which almost certainly occurred about 64 AD. The Gospel is usually dated around this time. Mark's reasons for writing must have been many and I can scarcely examine them in much detail here. It is clear, however, that he wished to prove that Jesus was the expected Messiah. Questions were being asked. How could a common criminal now be hailed as the Anointed One? Such a person could not have risen from the dead! Mark intended to set the record straight. He wrote for a community which was becoming increasingly unpopular and facing more and more persecution. The Gospel of Mark is not a Life of Jesus or a biography. Rather it is an attempt to explain how it was that Jesus preached the Kingdom, was transfigured, rejected, crucified and rose again for us. The Transfiguration comes very nearly in the middle of Mark's Gospel.

Mark 9:2–8

(2) Six days later, Jesus took with him Peter and James and John and led them up a high mountain on their own by themselves. (3) There in their presence he was transfigured: his clothes became brilliantly white, whiter than earthly bleacher could make them. (4) Elijah appeared to them with Moses; and they were talking to Jesus. (5) Then Peter spoke to Jesus, 'Rabbi', he said, 'it is wonderful for us to be here; so let us make three shelters, one for you, one for Moses, and one for Elijah.' (6) He did not know what to say; they were so frightened. (7) And a cloud came, covering them in shadow; and from the cloud there came a voice, 'This is my Son, the Beloved. Listen to him.' (8) Then suddenly, when they looked round, they saw no one with them any more but only Jesus.

Burkhill suggests that at this moment Mark 'evidently feels that the situation calls for some convincing demonstration of the reality of Messiahship'.[1] The revelation of Jesus as Messiah at Caesarea Philippi, followed by the dramatic demonstration of glory on the mountaintop and the divine vindication of Jesus by God the Father combine to bring to a climax all that Jesus has said and done in Galilee. The Transfiguration acts as a natural bridge in the Gospel between Jesus' teaching and healing ministry in Galilee and his passion in Jerusalem.

Mark the editor: the context

Mark was influenced by various people and sources but the final chronology of events in his Gospel was his own. Key incidents in Jesus' life obviously happened at particular moments. Geography also helped Mark put the jigsaw of Jesus' life together. He is particularly at home with geographical references within Galilee.

The Transfiguration comes shortly after Peter's confession of faith at Caesarea Philippi and the first prediction of his suffering; there is the warning in Mark 9:1 about the Kingdom of God coming in power followed by the Transfiguration story itself, and a further prediction of Jesus' passion. Stein explains the position of the Transfiguration narrative: 'In Mark the Transfiguration clearly serves the purpose of confirming Peter's confession and ratifying Jesus' prediction of his suffering and resurrection; and since the passion sayings are primarily Marcan redaction, the arrangement of the Transfiguration after Peter's Confession and the passion prediction serves Mark well.'[2]

The verses immediately before the Transfiguration are fascinating because of the way in which they focus on the nature of discipleship. There is a mention of the Messianic Secret idea (that Jesus does not yet want his identity too widely known) but the climax of this section is Peter's reply: 'You are the Christ.' It was the moment that Jesus had been waiting for. Mark 8:31–33 contains the first direct prediction by Jesus of his suffering in Jerusalem. There are three such prophecies before the passion. I will discuss these and their connection with the Transfiguration in a later chapter. Notice again, however, the prominence of Peter who rebukes Jesus for suggesting that he will suffer; Jesus in turn rebukes him. At Caesarea Philippi, in the prediction of Jesus' suffering, and on the mountain of the Transfiguration, the Gospel writer records Peter's prominence. Mark 8:34–38 then sets the scene for those who see the context of the

Transfiguration as that of the real test of discipleship. Once Peter has confessed Jesus as Messiah, the prediction of suffering is made. The need for all believers to share in that suffering is emphasised by Jesus.

Mark 9:1 has attracted most attention in discussion on the context of the Transfiguration in this Gospel: 'And he said to them, "In truth I tell you, there are some standing here who will not taste death before they see the kingdom of God come with power." ' In most translations of the Bible this verse is printed as part of the preceding section on discipleship rather than attached to the Transfiguration story. The origin of the verse remains a mystery. We cannot be certain if it was spoken by Jesus in this context. Those, such as Boobyer, who understand the Transfiguration as a vision of Jesus at his Second Coming believe that the verse has been chosen by Mark to highlight the point. But others believe that in the ministry of Jesus part of Mark 9:1 has already been fulfilled: 'some of those who heard Jesus speak before their deaths awake to the fact that the Kingdom of God has come'.[3] Some element of future expectation cannot be ruled out of any interpretation of Mark 9:1. The way in which the Peter source of the Transfiguration is used in 2 Peter (where the author is explaining why there is a delay in the Second Coming) adds weight to the belief that Mark edited his source into a context which was acceptable in the eyes of the Early Church.

The sections that follow the Transfiguration are just as interesting. Verses 9–13 record a conversation between Jesus and his disciples on the way back down the mountain. Jesus commands that his identity should remain secret (v.9) and then there is some rather confusing discussion about the coming of the Son of Man (v. 10–13). Dunn suggests that the selection by Mark of this conversation on the way down the mountain is 'unlikely to be accidental'[4] and it is true that these verses do indeed read like a real conversation between Jesus and his disciples. The reference to Elijah is interesting because it seems, on the evidence of these verses, that the Early Church expected the coming of Elijah before the dawning of the end of time. The disciples are complaining that since Elijah has not yet come the dawning of the final Age cannot be imminent.

Mark the editor: central motifs

The Transfiguration story in Mark is rich in theological imagery. Any serious study of the passage must acknowledge the difficulties involved in explaining such a varied and compact series of different motifs. Caird stated that Mark 9:2–8, 'our primary source, presents by itself a sufficiently complex problem of exegesis',[5] Taylor backed this up with the view that 'the narrative presents a very difficult problem and few will claim that they can give an explanation which completely satisfies them'.[6] Where a motif has a more prominent or powerful significance overall in either Matthew or Luke I will leave any detailed explanation until a later chapter. My aim here is to establish what the Transfiguration story meant for Mark the Evangelist. So I will now look briefly at each verse in turn and at those details which will help us to understand the Transfiguration.

v. 2 Six days later, Jesus took Peter and John and James and led them up a high mountain on their own by themselves.

A reference to a specific period of time – 'six days' – in Mark is rare. In the first eight chapters he displays no real interest in the passing of time during Jesus' Galilean ministry. It is not clear whether Mark is suggesting that the Transfiguration of Jesus took place six days after the events in Caesarea Philippi or whether he has used this number because it has a special significance. The former seems more likely. The prominence of Peter both at Ceasarea and on the Transfiguration mountain adds weight to the idea that Peter himself was Mark's main source. It is not impossible that the chronological connection of 'six days' was part of the Peter source. The main problem with this argument is that Luke changes the number of days from six to eight. But if Mark was wanting to say 'about a week later' the use of six or eight days would hardly be significant in itself.

Certain numbers do have a special significance in the

Bible. In Exodus 24:16, for instance, we read: 'The Glory of Yahweh rested on Mount Sinai and the cloud covered it for six days.' It is not inconceivable that Mark was reminding us of this momentous event in the Old Testament. The glory and the cloud are also present in that story. Some scholars have suggested a reference here to the 'Day of the Lord', but this is highly unlikely. Reference to the passing of 'days' in the New Testament is often linked to the resurrection of Jesus, and Bultmann uses this argument to draw parallels. But the phrase 'six days' has no parallel in the resurrection stories. Instead it is almost certainly a reference to the amount of time that elapsed between Peter's confession at Ceasarea Philippi and the events on the mountain.

The fact that Jesus took Peter, James and John with him reveals something of the importance of this event from the point of view of Jesus himself. There is no article before John's name in the original Greek and this has the effect of linking him more closely with James. In other words, Peter, along with James and John, are taken to the summit of the mountain. The Transfiguration is not the only time these three are grouped together. They are the first three disciples to be named by Mark (3:16–17). When Jesus heals the official's daughter he allows no one to follow him except Peter, James and John (5:37). In the Garden of Gethsemane the same three are present. Dr Bruce Chilton believes that this inner cabinet of disciples is not a result of Mark's role as editor 'but that a select group of three was a part of the tradition accepted by the Early Church'.[7] The plural 'we' in 2 Peter might not have been spelt out as Peter, James and John because the Early Church took this for granted. But the selection of these three disciples out of the wider group of twelve enables Jesus to show them the whole mystery of the glory which God had revealed in his own person. The presence of Peter, James and John on the mountain sets the scene for Mark to demonstrate how important is the path of discipleship.

Farrer's suggestion that the disciples experience a picture of Jesus as Messiah to give them confidence and conviction for the future is important here: 'The Transfiguration is the calling of the three apostolic witnesses to the full exercise of their function and as such it takes place in the series of apostolic scenes'.[8] Their presence on the mountain enables them to see the glory of God made visible in Christ and this is to become an essential part of their apostolic witness concerning the revelation of Christ in the world. To be a disciple of Jesus means that we must recognise him as Messiah and, in order to experience the glory of Jesus in our own lives, we must continually come down from the mountain and face whatever suffering and uncertainty the world may throw at us. But the glory remains constant. Christ remains the Messiah. Suffering has been transfigured. The venue of the Transfiguration – a high and lonely mountain – will be looked at more closely in the next chapter when I study Matthew's account.

> **v. 3** There in their presence he was transfigured: his clothes became brilliantly white, whiter than any earthly bleacher could make them.

The idea of transfiguration appears rarely in the Bible. The verb 'to be transfigured' does not appear at all in the Old Testament. The shining of Moses' face (Exodus 34:29ff.) and the vision in Daniel (10:5ff.) can be described as transfiguration experiences without the verb actually being used. Many scholars believe that the idea of transfiguration was more common in Pagan circles and that some elements of Jewish expectation latched on to this (2 Baruch 51:3; Enoch 38:4, 104:2). The Greek verb 'to be transfigured' (*metamorphousthai*) occurs only four times in the New Testament of which this, in Mark, is one. It literally means 'assumed a different form'. The verb also appears in Matthew's account of the Transfiguration, in Romans 12:2 and in 2 Corinthians 3:10. The fact that Luke chooses not to use the verb is interesting and I will examine this later. Cranfield draws a clear distinction between the Gospel use of the verb where a *temporary* glimpse of the glory of God is inferred and Paul's understanding of an *abiding* glory.

In choosing the title of his book, *The Glory of God and the Transfiguration of Christ*, Archbishop Michael Ramsey was

31

making an important point. The concept of transfiguration, a dramatic change from one state to another, was inextricably linked to the revelation of the Divine Glory. *The chief significance of the Transfiguration of Jesus lies in the fact that the Glory of God was revealed to the disciples.* This is made even more dramatic when the clothes of Jesus become whiter than any fuller on earth could bleach them. Mark omits the detail that Jesus' face was also shining; this is added later by Matthew and Luke. Matthew obviously sees this as important, bearing in mind the experience of Moses (Exodus 34:29ff.). Shining garments and whiteness both have Old Testament and apocalyptic backgrounds. The Hebrew word *kavod*, meaning glory, is extremely common. Ramsey suggests that 'kavod denotes the revealed being or character of the Lord and also a physical phenomenon whereby Yahweh's presence is made known.'[9] As I mentioned in the opening chapter, the Orthodox tradition links the transfiguration state with the concept of light. God is revealed as light on the Transfiguration mountain in the same way that St John describes the light in 8:12: 'I am the light of the world; anyone who follows me will not be walking in the dark but will have the light of life.' Timothy Ware suggests: 'This divine light, seen by the three disciples on the mountain – seen also by many of the saints during prayer – is nothing else than the uncreated energies of God.'[10] Another way of describing the uncreated energies would be to suggest that the glory of God is revealed in the person of Christ in a dramatic and totally convincing way. In being transfigured, Jesus embodies the glory of God in his innermost being.

So the Transfiguration consisted of a visual demonstration of Jesus' messianic glory. And, following the explanations of Boobyer, it is not impossible that 'the transfiguration was to Mark a vision, given beforehand, of Jesus as he will be at his second advent.'[11] Peter had confessed Jesus as Messiah at Ceasarea and now that Messiahship is confirmed in this transfiguration experience. The suffering that Jesus had already spoken about would be transfigured by the glory of God.

v. 4 Elijah appeared to them with Moses; and they were talking to Jesus.

I will examine the significance of the presence of Moses and Elijah in the next chapter. Mark suggests that Jesus, Moses and Elijah were engaged in conversation. It is possible that Peter provided this information to Mark though there is no reference to the two figures in the 2 Peter account. It may be, however, that the eyewitnesses mentioned in 2 Peter included Moses and Elijah and that this was well known in the Early Church. Margaret Thrall warns against treating the figures of Moses and Elijah as 'peripheral and additional symbols'.[12] She believes that the two figures are centrally important and that their role needs to be examined more closely. She insists: 'They are not merely part of the symbolic background scenery. In some senses they are figures upon whom the whole story turns.'[13] That Moses and Elijah are witnesses of the divine glory is indisputable. It is also obvious that in some way they place Jesus in his proper context: two great figures of the Old Testament are present on his right and left to witness the divine glory which is placed in him and on him by God.

v. 5 Then Peter spoke to Jesus, 'Rabbi', he said, 'it is wonderful for us to be here; so let us make three shelters, one for you, one for Moses and one for Elijah.'

The theme of discipleship returns to centre stage in this verse. It is Peter who is under the spotlight. Peter exclaims what a wonderful privilege it is for the three disciples to be present at such a moment and his words 'It is good to be here' are perhaps the best known. To be a disciple of Jesus at this moment means joy and happiness. Once again, Peter is the spokesman for the disciples. Rawlinson submits that he must be in a dream or a trance to suggest what he does.[14] As early as 1909, Bacon[15] pointed out that Peter is frequently referred to in terms of rebuke or disgrace (cf. 8:27ff.; 10:28ff.; 14:25ff.; 14:66–72). Other commentators agree but stress that by 64 AD Peter was already highly

33

regarded and there was no need to protect or build up his image.

Bruce Chilton believes that this verse heightens the theme of discipleship. The Transfiguration is 'an experience of the disciples rather than of Jesus himself ... a vision experienced by the disciples'.[16] The use of the term 'Rabbi' is also interesting. In using it Mark prepared the way for Peter to suggest the building of three tabernacles. Our own understanding of the term is rather different from that of the New Testament period. In Jesus' day the title would have suggested someone who commanded respect from ordinary people; the scribes were often addressed in this way or a pupil could use it of his teacher. Jesus is addressed as Rabbi by Nicodemus (John 3:2), Nathaniel (John 1:49), Judas (Matthew 26:25,49) and elsewhere by Peter (for example, Mark 11:21). The other disciples and groups of people are also reported to have addressed Jesus in this way (John 1:28; 4:3; 6:25; 9:2; 11:8; 14:45). But Matthew substitutes Rabbi with Lord in the Transfiguration story and Luke changes the title to Master. In Mark the use of Rabbi underlines the idea that Peter perceived that Jesus was to be revered and was now equal in stature to Moses and Elijah who had appeared with him. The role of the disciple was to learn from the teacher.

This leads us conveniently to the question of Peter's suggestion that three tabernacles should be constructed. The best-known explanation is that Peter wanted, in some way, to prolong the scene. The tabernacles were to be built for Jesus, Moses and Elijah. We are not told what provision Peter suggested should be made for the three disciples. Perhaps Peter had in mind verses such as Joel 3:21 and Zechariah 2:10ff. where it was expected that God would once more pitch his tent when the Day of the Lord arrived. The Feast of Tabernacles is one of the most important Jewish festivals celebrated each year as a reminder of the forty years in the wilderness. In some circles it had assumed a role in Jewish expectation relating to the Messiah's coming. Peter obviously had in mind the notion of God dwelling with his people in the person of Jesus and the presence of Moses and Elijah is in keeping with this essentially Old Testament idea of tents or tabernacles. It is not impossible, however, that we should understand this also partly in a futuristic sense: the tents would be a sign that God had come to rest with his people in Christ for ever. Peter's prominence and expression of delight at the scene he witnessed emphasised his joy at being a part of the revelation of the Son of God at that time and in that place.

v. 6 He did not know what to say; they were so frightened.

This is a direct reminiscence of St Peter and there is a natural link with Mark 14:40: 'And once more Jesus came back and found them sleeping, their eyes were so heavy and they could find no answer for him.' Peter, as Mark's source, remembers this very human feeling as he watches the Transfiguration take place. Although this is not recorded in the 2 Peter account, there is no reason why Peter could not have added this gloss at a later stage. It is in no way essential to the account. Peter is simply seen as a spokesman for the disciples and one who is essentially vulnerable like all of us. This verse reinforces the notion that the Transfiguration of Jesus was primarily for the disciples: that Jesus might be truly revealed as the Messiah of God.

v. 7 And a cloud came, covering them in shadow; and from the cloud there came a voice, 'This is my Son, the Beloved. Listen to him.'

This verse emphasises the theme of discipleship because it contains a divine command that the disciples listen to what Jesus is saying. The voice of God confirms Jesus' messianic role as the Son of God. It is obvious that Mark intended us to see a direct link between the baptism of Jesus in 1:9–11 and the Transfiguration where God also speaks. The theological significance to readers of a cloud and a voice would have been rooted in the fact that both of these were prominent in the Old Testament and Jewish expectation. I will examine both the cloud and the voice in greater detail in my consideration of the Matthew and Luke accounts. In Matthew both have strong Old Testament connotations. Luke effectively links them to his use of the word *doxa* – glory.

If the 2 Peter account of the Transfiguration is based on a Peter source it is one without any reference to a cloud. But this can easily be explained as editorial work by Mark who wanted to strengthen the similarity between the baptism and the Transfiguration stories. Whether a cloud actually appeared on the mountain or whether this was a development of later tradition is a matter for ongoing debate. The cloud is a symbol of present revelation and future glory. It is the vehicle which God uses and through which he speaks. God reveals his pleasure in what is taking place through the cloud which points to a new exodus, the birth of a new people of God and future glory. Mark suggests that the voice speaks from the cloud. The fact that there is a voice in 2 Peter 1:17 suggests that it was definitely a part of the apostolic tradition coming directly from Peter from a very early period. Once again there are strong theological connections between the voice and the Old Testament as well as a clear role in Jewish expectation.

In Mark the voice denotes divine presence. God is present with his Son, the Old Testament witnesses and the disciples on the holy mountain. God speaks to them. Riesenfeld believes that the voice has the same function in both the baptism and the Transfiguration stories: 'it reveals the relationship between Father and Son',[17] underlining the divine authority by which Jesus acts and speaks. Other scholars see the voice as the basic link between the two stories, but Bernadin makes the interesting point that whilst, by the River Jordan, only Jesus hears the Father's voice, at the Transfiguration the voice is directed at the disciples.[18] This emphasises the idea that Mark intends the disciples to comprehend the nature of Jesus' life and mission through the experience of transfiguration. As well as references to God's voice in the baptism and the Transfiguration narratives, the voice of God also has a revealing purpose in the Fourth Gospel. God is said to reveal his purpose through the voice (John 3:8) and the voice is also linked to the idea of personal salvation.

But it is the *words* spoken by the voice that are most important: 'This is my beloved son, Listen to him.' The drama of God himself vindicating Jesus' true status should not be overlooked. The message is very close to that preserved in the 2 Peter account. After Peter has confessed Jesus as Messiah at Caesarea Philippi this bold statement from God himself leaves the disciples in no doubt whatsoever who Jesus was. Human nature is such that when the disciples were put under pressure after the arrest of Jesus the memory of the Transfiguration temporarily evaded them, particularly when Peter denied ever having known Jesus. But as the disciples pondered everything, this majestic sight must have left them in no doubt that Jesus of Nazareth embodied the glory of God who confirmed his sonship from a cloud that overshadowed them. The command of God to listen to Jesus is a pertinent one. Life is so full of noise and words. So often we think of praying as reading out a long list of petitions, thoughts and anxieties to God. Learning to listen to what Jesus has to say to us in our daily lives is one of the main lessons of discipleship. It is something that we all need to do.

v. 8 Then suddenly, when they looked round, they saw no one with them any more but only Jesus.

It was over. After the drama of the event the conclusion came quickly. Following the descriptions of the transfigured Jesus, the appearance of Moses and Elijah and the intervention of God by his voice through a cloud, Mark uses this verse as a bridge between the narrative itself and the conversation of Jesus with his disciples on the way back down the mountain.

Mark the editor: the Transfiguration

The central theme of Mark's story is the importance and significance of *discipleship*. The glory is revealed for the sake of the disciples, that they might see Jesus in his true relationship with God who speaks directly to him. Kenney believes that this is especially clear when a comparison is made between the Transfiguration story and the betrayal of Jesus in the Garden of Gethsemane.[19] The same three disciples are there and the same phrase – 'they did not know what to say for they were afraid' – appears in the Gospel (9:6 and 14:40). Kenney argues that this underlines the central theme of discipleship: 'they are two of the most significant episodes of our Lord's revelation of himself to his disciples.' The divine glory was revealed to those who had begun to understand the significance of Jesus' coming into the world.

The Transfiguration was an encouragement to the disciples about their long-term future. Boobyer's view that the Transfiguration is an anticipation of the Second Coming is partly rooted in his understanding of Mark's account. He believes that St Mark's Gospel is essentially futuristic, 'looking forward to some great day of future revelation'.[20] Pointing to various passages, Boobyer believes that the Transfiguration has a comfortable place in Mark's Gospel because it points forward to the glory that will be revealed finally and completely in the future. Baptism in the Holy Spirit (1:8), predictions of his passion and his own future (8:31; 9:31; 10:34) and futuristic material of another kind (9:9; 10:37; 14:25–38) are further evidence that the theological significance of the Transfiguration in the Gospel of Mark always looks to the future. To this extent, the disciples of Jesus are helped to understand something of the faith, hope and confidence which Jesus embodies in his glorified presence on the mountain. Discipleship is about a confident hope in the future; it is about the reality of glory triumphing over evil and sin in the long term.

But before that future hope can become a reality the task of discipleship is also to share fully in the suffering of Jesus during our earthly life. Jesus, as Son of God and Son of Man, demands that we take up our cross and follow him so that we can share in that glory now and in the future. The authority by which Jesus fulfils his task is rooted firmly in God the Father, and Mark is careful to draw together the baptism and the Transfiguration stories within his Gospel. In both stories Jesus is seen as the chosen one, the one appointed by God, the Messiah. The Baptism 'provides the introduction to an understanding of the whole life of Jesus – and of all Christology. Who is Jesus?' and his unique role in salvation history is then revealed.[21] Cullmann adds: 'It is certainly no accident that the words from heaven at the transfiguration repeat those of the heavenly voice at the baptism.' We are disciples of the Son of God whose authority rests with God.

I have already stressed the connection between Caesarea Philippi and the Transfiguration; this is another passage that helps us to understand the nature of discipleship in the light of the events on the mountain. Most scholars regard the Transfiguration as a dramatic illustration of Peter's response to Jesus' question at Caesarea.

> 'Who do people say I am?' And they told him, John the Baptist, others Elijah, others again, one of the prophets. 'But you,' he asked them, 'who do you say I am?' Peter spoke up and said to him, 'You are the Christ.' And he gave them strict orders not to tell anyone about him. (Mark 8:27–30)

Peter's response of 'You are the Christ' is visibly demonstrated on the mountain of the Transfiguration and the disciple's understanding of who Jesus was is obviously transformed in the process. Peter's role, as the one who always speaks out, is repeated and the call to secrecy in both passages also ties the two stories together. The Transfiguration is thus a symbolic vision of Peter's confession of faith at Caesarea. Jesus is the Son of God, the glorious Messiah: Peter confesses him as such and then sees the reality of this for himself. Discipleship is never an easy option in Mark's Gospel.

4. Wrapped up in Mystery: the Gospel of Matthew

Appearing together with Jesus, Moses and Elijah sum up the entire drama of the Old Covenant and point to Jesus as its consummator. (A. M. Hunter)[1]

We come now to the second account of the Transfiguration of Jesus in the Gospels. Early tradition usually names Matthew the apostle as the author. Scholars now propose that Matthew wrote a Hebrew Gospel which was translated at a later date by a scribe or by Matthew himself. Most believe that the Gospel as we now have it was written in the last decade of the first century. Until the nineteenth century Matthew was always regarded as the first Gospel but commentators are now almost unanimous in their belief that Matthew was heavily reliant on Mark. The author has a deep knowledge of Judaism and can be best described as a 'Jewish Christian'. David Hill believes that the Jewish background to Matthew's Gospel is absolutely fundamental to our understanding of the evangelist's message: 'The most immediately striking characteristic of Matthew's Gospel is what may be loosely termed its "Jewishness". The formula-quotations [the direct quotations from the Old Testament throughout the Gospel of Matthew] clearly emphasise the fulfilment of scriptural prophecies in the person and work of Jesus and are therefore obviously intended to prove that Jesus is the goal of the Old Testament revelation of God.'[2]

Matthew's is a much longer Gospel than Mark's and it focuses keenly on the concept of the Kingdom of Heaven. The coming of the Kingdom is equated with the fact that the law and the prophets have been fulfilled in the person of Jesus the Messiah. Matthew quotes regularly from the Old Testament. Much of the imagery of the Transfiguration has added meaning for Matthew because he writes with a Jewish understanding of the symbols and motifs, many of which have a long and significant Old Testament background, as Harald Riesenfeld underlines in his book *Jésus Transfiguré.*[3] As we reflect on Matthew's understanding of the Transfiguration we need to bear in mind his overall view that in Jesus we see the Old Testament expectation being fulfilled in the Messiah of God. The glory of God which was revealed to the people of God many times in the Old Testament is now presented finally and completely in the person of Jesus. Let us look more closely at the Transfiguration in Matthew.

Matthew 17:1–8

(1) Six days later, Jesus took with him Peter and James and his brother John and led them up a high mountain, by themselves. (2) There in their presence he was transfigured: his face shone like the sun and his clothes became as dazzling as light. (3) And suddenly Moses and Elijah appeared to them; they were talking with him. (4) Then Peter spoke to Jesus, 'Lord', he said, 'it is wonderful for us to be here; if you want me to, I will make three shelters here, one for you, one for Moses and one for Elijah.' (5) He was still speaking when suddenly a bright cloud covered them with shadow, and suddenly from the cloud there came a voice which said, 'This is my Son, the Beloved; he enjoys my favour. Listen to him.' (6) When they heard this, the disciples fell on their faces, overcome with fear. (7) But Jesus came up and touched them, saying, 'Stand up, do not be afraid.' (8) And when they raised their eyes they saw no one but Jesus.

St Matthew includes nearly all of Mark's story but the Transfiguration in Matthew has a distinctly different feel to it. There is an immediate sense of the Old Testament being fulfilled both in the Matthew story of the Transfiguration and in its Gospel context. The main difference in detail between Mark and Matthew concerns the fear of the disciples on seeing the transfigured Jesus: he places their expression of fear *after* the divine voice has intervened rather than before. This further reinforces the idea of discipleship being a response to the calling of God which I referred to in Mark's Gospel. The Transfiguration is placed in a sequence of events in Matthew in a very similar way to that of Mark. The confession of faith of Peter at Caesarea Philippi (16:13ff.) is followed by Jesus' prediction of his sufferings in Jerusalem (v. 21ff.). Before the Transfiguration story Jesus outlines the path of true discipleship (v. 24ff). On the way down the mountain questions are asked concerning the coming of Elijah (17:9ff.). Matthew has obviously been influenced by Mark's ordering of events.

v. 1 Six days later, Jesus took with him Peter and James and his brother John and led them up a high mountain, by themselves.

A high mountain was a particularly appropriate setting for the Transfiguration to the Jewish-Christian readers of St Matthew; mountains were places of revelation in Judaism as well as in other religions. It may well have reminded Matthew's readers of Moses taking Aaron, Nadab and Abihu with him to the top of the holy mountain in Exodus 24:1. The mountain is the venue in the 2 Peter account as well as in all three of the Synoptic Gospels and, as I mentioned in Chapter 1, there has been widespread debate about which mountain it was. If we take the Gospel sequence seriously it must be one within six days' walking distance of Caesarea Philippi. Most scholars agree that we shall never know for certain, but Kopp (who writes that the identity of the mountain is 'wrapped up in mystery'[4]) suggests that Mount Tabor could easily have been reached within that time. He also believes that Mark 9:30 ('They went on from there and passed through Galilee') adds weight to the case for Tabor. The other candidate is Mount Hermon which is further to the north. Michael Ramsey believed that it would have been a more isolated and therefore a likelier site.[5] In the end we must rely on conjecture.

Many religions in the Middle East regarded the mountain as a sacred or special place. The Samaritans, for example, believed that the Garizim was their sacred mountain. In Babylonian mythology mountains were the birthplaces of various gods. In the Jewish tradition the mountain's central function is as a place of revelation. At key moments in the history of Israel God communicates with his people on a mountain. Thus Isaac was to be offered as Abraham's sacrifice upon a mountain (Genesis 22:2); during battle, Moses is reported to have prayed to the Lord on the top of a mountain (Exodus 17:9); Elijah prays on the summit of Mount Carmel (1 Kings 18:42). The Hebrew tradition clearly associated the mountain with the presence of God. It provided the stage for God's revelation to the world (see also Psalm 2:6; 15:1; 43:3; Isaiah 2:2; 27:13; 66:20). Most commentators believe that this Old Testament understanding of the mountain was in the mind of the evangelists as they recorded the Transfiguration story. It is in many ways a visionary experience akin to Exodus 24 on Mount Sinai. The mountain is also a venue in a variety of incidents in the New Testament (for example, Matthew 4:8; 5:1; 15:23; 26:30; Mark 3:13ff.). Here it is frequently associated with a desire on the part of Jesus for solitude or isolation, particularly if he feels the need to pray. Riesenfeld colourfully describes the mountain in the New Testament as the 'théâtre, où se déroule l'action' (a theatre where the action takes place).

In some Rabbinic literature the mountain is cited as the expected venue for the Second Coming, when the Day of the Lord would be revealed, and there are some New Testament passages where such an understanding is likely (Matthew 24:3; Mark 13:3; Revelation 21:20). The mountain is basically the place of revelation. On Mount Tabor the law and the prophets are fulfilled in the coming of Jesus who is glorified by God. It is the ultimate revelation to those present that the Kingdom of Heaven is at hand. And it sets the scene for subsequent events in Jerusalem when the glory would be perfected in the resurrection. Matthew also agrees with Mark that the event took place six days after the dramatic confession of Peter at Caesarea Philippi. The reference to six days could also be connected with Exodus 24:16 where God speaks to Moses on Sinai 'after six days'. The number of days will be discussed again in the next chapter.

v. 2 There in their presence he was transfigured: his face shone like the sun and his clothes became as dazzling as light.

Matthew differs slightly in his description of the transfigured Jesus. The fact that Jesus' face 'shone like the sun' and that his clothes became 'as dazzling as light' are unique to this Gospel. The description is similar to Mark's but the verse feels different. There is a strong parallel here with Moses' face shining on Mount Sinai (Exodus 34:29ff.); there his face shone with a reflection of the glory of God. The main difference in the Transfiguration story is that the cloud does not contain the glory, as it does in the Old Testament. The cloud in the Transfiguration appears later. Matthew seems keen to emphasise the sheer brightness of the revelation of God's glory on the mountain. The divine glory is embodied within the person of Jesus and the disciples bear witness to it. It is a tremendous scene which contrasts sharply with the despair of Jesus on the cross.

v. 3 And suddenly Moses and Elijah appeared to them; they were talking with him.

Moses and Elijah play a key role in Matthew's Transfiguration story. These two great figures of the Old Testament, who are so well known to Matthew's readers, appear with Jesus on the holy mountain. In Mark we are told that Elijah and Moses appeared; in Matthew (and Luke) the order is reversed. The presence of Elijah is conceivably easier to justify than that of Moses. During the inter-testamental period and in Rabbinic Judaism, Elijah was expected to play a major role in future and final events. He would deliver Israel in the last days from the wrath that would affect her. He would also be the forerunner of the Messiah and the High Priest of the Messianic age. To this extent many believed that John the Baptist was Elijah (John 1:21, 25) and, following the ministry of John the Baptist, Elijah's appearance on the mountain would hardly have surprised those present. He would have been associated with the beginning of the end of time.

Whereas Elijah clearly had a role to play in this context

Moses is rarely portrayed as an apocalyptic figure in the New Testament. Indeed, the role of Moses in the New Testament is confusing and sometimes contradictory. In considering Moses' presence on the Transfiguration mountain it is important to begin with the notion of Moses as the giver of the law in the Old Testament, with Jesus acting, in some way, as a natural fulfilment of all that was promised in the Torah. Deuteronomy 18:15 is a particularly potent verse: 'The Lord will raise up for you a prophet like me from among you, from your brethren – him shall you heed.' There are two clear alternatives available to us as we interpret this verse. On the one hand it is reasonable to think not of one individual prophet but of a succession of prophets throughout the ages, culminating in the Messiah. But on the other hand there is abundant evidence in Jewish expectation pointing to the anticipated Messiah as a 'new' or 'second' Moses.

The most conservative interpretation of the appearance of Moses and Elijah on the Transfiguration mountain is given by those who believe that the two represent the law and the prophets. Commentators are divided on this. Some suggest that no representative role existed anywhere else in religious thought, whilst others argue that Moses could not represent the law at all. In fact, the opposite is true. Moses is there to confirm the fulfilment of the Torah in the person of Jesus and to bear witness to the coming of the Messiah. Boobyer has produced the neatest conclusion this century: 'They can fittingly belong to a story understood by Mark as a confirmation of Christ's Messiahship in the form of a prediction of his Second Coming.'[6] In other words, Moses and Elijah appear with the transfigured Lord to confirm his status as Son of God and Messiah in a context underlining the notion that Christ will return at some time in the future. Tasker stresses the importance of their homage to Jesus: 'the primary purpose of the appearance of Moses and Elijah was to salute their divine Successor and then to leave Him alone in His unchallenged supremacy, the sole object of His disciples' veneration.'[7]

v. 4 Then Peter spoke to Jesus, 'Lord,' he said, 'it is wonderful

45

for us to be here; if you want me to, I will make three shelters here, one for you, one for Moses and one for Elijah.'

Once again, as in Mark, Peter's comment 'It is wonderful for us to be here' gives the Transfiguration story a distinctly human touch. Peter's suggestion, that he should build three tabernacles, would have been particularly poignant since the Feast of Tabernacles was an extremely important occasion in the religious calendar. In fulfilling what was expected of the Messiah in terms of Judaism, Peter attempts to prolong the scene of glory; but the story moves on quickly. The Greek word *skene* translates the Hebrew word for 'a pointed tent'. The term later applied to the tabernacle which was a movable place of worship erected in the wilderness wherever the worshipping community gathered. The same word could be used for the leafy booths which the Israelites constructed during the Feast of Tabernacles to use as shelters. Frequently, when I am travelling in the Holy Land today, I notice the tents of the Bedouins, authentic nomads who live in the desert and who move around according to the climate, the wind direction and the availability of water. The early desert dwellers would have done the same.

Peter is referring to the shelters used at the Feast of Tabernacles and Matthew's readers would have been well acquainted with this harvest celebration. It looked back to Israel's journey through the wilderness and celebrated the sovereignty of God. It also looked forward to a time when all nations would worship with Israel, praising God for his wonderful works. Commentators have spent far too long agonising over whether Peter intended the shelters for Jesus, Moses and Elijah or for the three disciples. In Mark the answer is clear and we can be content with the explanation that Peter simply wanted to prolong the scene and build three shelters for Jesus and the witnesses of this divine revelation. Riesenfeld believes that this verse emphasises the idea that the Transfiguration is principally concerned with the fulfilment of Old Testament expectation. Peter was stunned; having just confessed Jesus as Messiah at Caesarea Philippi, this was almost too much. Not sure of what he is saying, he makes reference to a well-known shelter in a religious festival with which he would have been well acquainted.

> **v. 5** He was still speaking when suddenly a bright cloud covered them with shadow, and suddenly from the cloud there came a voice which said, 'This is my Son, the Beloved; he enjoys my favour. Listen to him.'

The cloud and the voice are central to the drama of the Transfiguration story. The glory of God is revealed and Matthew clearly believes that the disciples now understand what is taking place. Both of these motifs have a strong Old Testament history and in Matthew's account this background is particularly noticeable. Parallels between the appearance of a cloud at the Transfiguration and the baptism are obvious and were explored in the last chapter. In the Old Testament the cloud can easily be identified with the appearance of God to his people, especially in scenes which are generally regarded as moments of great revelation.

> Cloud covered the mountain. The glory of the Lord rested on Mount Sinai and the cloud covered it for six days. On the seventh day the Lord called to Moses from inside the cloud. To the watching Israelites, the glory of the Lord looked like a devouring fire on the mountain top. Moses went right into the cloud and went on up the mountain. Moses stayed on the mountain for forty days and forty nights. (Exodus 24:15–18)

A cloud was often present when God appeared to his people. And in much later apocalyptic thought the cloud was similarly associated with the appearance of God. 'I was gazing into the visions of the night, when I saw, coming on the clouds of heaven, as it were, a son of man.' (Daniel 7:13)

In terms of Jesus' Second Coming the cloud had a definite role to play within the New Testament itself (for example, 13:26; 14:62; Revelation 1:7; 14:14). It is also the case that a cloud features in the story of Jesus' ascension (Acts 1:9ff.). And so the cloud implies the revelation of an important message with God's presence stamped upon it. There is also a link between the idea of revealed glory and a cloud. This is embodied in the idea of *shekinah* – a Hebrew word

47

denoting God's presence of dwelling in glory. We see this perfectly in the transfigured Jesus: the cloud is a symbol of present revelation and future glory.

Matthew would have been fully aware of the Old Testament, eschatological and apocalyptic background. The cloud was the vehicle by which God made himself known. It links the idea of Transfiguration and the Second Coming but the glorious scene is only a temporary glimpse of what will be revealed finally and perfectly at some future time. Sabourin summarises the cloud's function here perfectly: 'The cloud in the Transfiguration is, without doubt, a theophanic cloud from which God speaks as his dwelling place. Its apparition and its function on the mountain point to a new exodus, to a new revelation, to the birth of a new people of God, that of End Time.'[8]

It is the voice of God that speaks from the cloud and readers of St Matthew's Gospel would have been familiar with the idea of God speaking directly in this way. In the Septuagint *phone* usually translates the Hebrew *kol,* which frequently denoted the voice of thunder (for example, Exodus 9:23, 29, 33ff.; 19:16; 20:18; Job 28:26), the roar of water (for example Psalm 42:7; 93:3ff.) or even the crackling of fire (Jeremiah 11:16). The most popular and well-known meaning of the Hebrew word denotes either a human voice or the voice of God. These references are most common in the descriptions of the wilderness wanderings where the voice of God signifies his presence and his dealings with his people (for example, Dueteronomy 5:4; 9:15; Exodus 3:2). And so the intelligible voice of God speaks to the people and his will is made known to them.

> Louder and louder grew the trumpeting. Moses spoke and God answered him in the thunder. (Exodus 19:19)

> 'Speak to us yourself,' they said to Moses 'and we will obey; but do not let God speak to us or we shall die.' (Exodus 20:19)

As with the cloud, the voice assumed a role in the future revelation of God at the coming of the Messiah. In Rabbinic Judaism there are many references to the voice of God speaking of the final coming of his chosen one. Here the *bat kol* represents the voice of God in judgement over his people. In the Synoptic Gospels the voice of God first appears in the baptism narratives. In Mark 1:11, we read: 'And a voice came from heaven, "You are my Son, the Beloved; my favour rests on you." ' The voice here confirms the unique relationship between God and his Son. Most scholars agree that the Gospel writers have edited their material to make sure that the reader sees a direct parallel between baptism and Transfiguration. Both are key events, at the beginning and the end of Jesus' Galilean ministry. Both are endorsed by the divine voice. The words 'This is my Son, the Beloved; he enjoys my favour' are similar to the words recorded by the author of 2 Peter. The divine command is that we should listen to Jesus. A verse from Deuteronomy inevitably springs to mind here: 'Yahweh your God will raise up for you a prophet like me; you will listen to him' (18:15).

Both the cloud and the voice have their roots firmly in Old Testament understanding and history. And yet they also point forward to the work that Christ has to do – the need to gain victory over suffering and death – to the power of the resurrection and the glorious Second Coming. God intervenes directly, telling the disciples to listen to what Jesus is saying. When God affirms Jesus as his Son on the mountain of the Transfiguration, a tremendous act of vindication takes place. In accord with the revelation of the Old Testament and the promise of a Messiah, God affirms that in Christ the Lord of all Life has come. Here, transformed in and through his glory, Jesus is revealed to his disciples and God gives him authority.

> **v. 6** When they heard this, the disciples fell on their faces, overcome with fear.

Fear is one way of describing the way we feel when we are directly confronted by God. In Matthew's account there is a sense of awe and bewilderment amongst the disciples following the Transfiguration. There was a clear need for the disciples to love Christ because of who he was and what he was doing. But their inability to understand fully what was happening results in a sense of fear and panic. Peter had confessed Jesus as Messiah at Caesarea Philippi so, in a way, none of the disciples should have been surprised that the authority of Jesus was now confirmed and emphasised by this glorious scene. But the humanity of the disciples as they face this powerful vision head-on is very strong indeed.

v. 7 But Jesus came up and touched them, saying, 'Stand up, do not be afraid.'

The response of Jesus here is unique to the Gospel of Matthew but it is similar to other passages. His basic command that they should have no fear reminds us of many other occasions, including Jairus' daughter (Mark 5:36) and Peter's fishes (Luke 5:10). Jesus understands their response but he does not feel that it is necessary for them to be fearful.

The Greek word *phobos* is one of those words you do not forget when learning New Testament Greek. It can be translated as terror, fear, alarm or fright, but it can also mean reverence, awe and respect. There is a distinct difference between Jewish and Hellenistic understanding of 'fearing God' and readers of St Matthew's Gospel would have been well acquainted with the former. Fear of God is a basic aspect of Jewish piety. A believer can stand before God in fear and in love (Genesis 15:1; Judges 6:23; Isaiah 44:2) for God is great and mighty and terrible, but he is also gracious to the believer who turns to him. Fear always results in acceptance.

This Jewish response to the love of God is much in evidence throughout the writings of the New Testament (Luke 18:2,4; Acts 9:31; 1 Peter 2:17). And when Jesus says 'Fear not' he is reminding his followers that, as in generations past, God's grace will give them the strength and the willpower to continue in faith. This is a theme that St Paul takes up in many of his Epistles, along with some of the other New Testament writers. 'In love there is no room for fear, but perfect love drives out fear, because fear implies punishment and whoever is afraid has not come to perfection in love.' (1 John 4:18) The fear of the disciples is perfectly understandable. But Jesus reminds them that God's grace will strengthen them and encourage them in their faith.

v. 8 And when they raised their eyes they saw no one but Jesus.

The Transfiguration was over. Moses and Elijah had departed. The task of Jesus remained: his journey to Jerusalem had to continue. The vision probably lasted only for a few minutes but now, after Peter's confession of Jesus as Messiah at Caesarea Philippi, the three disciples had seen for themselves the divine glory on the holy mountain. The scene was a temporal one and the reality of Jerusalem lay ahead, with the promise of suffering before the glory could be perfectly revealed.

The message of Matthew

The Transfiguration in the Gospel of Matthew provides us with new insights and understanding. David Hill believes that Matthew had the same purpose as Mark when he wrote down the Transfiguration story but he did so with different perceptions and from a different background. Jesus the Messiah is revealed in majesty, according to the expectation of the Jewish tradition. Dr Hill has highlighted a progression which may have taken place in the thought of the Early Church concerning the divine function of Jesus and which helps us to understand how the Church's concept of Jesus evolved. He points to three stages which are essential in any attempt to unravel the question of who Jesus is: the first is the historical ministry of Jesus, the second is the post-Easter period and the third is that of 'End Time'.

Matthew understands the Transfiguration as encapsulating all of these. The ministry of Jesus and his proclamation of the Kingdom of God results in his suffering, death and resurrection. Throughout the drama of Jesus' life and preaching there is a constant tension between the Old Covenant being fulfilled, the 'now' and the 'not yet'. In many ways the Transfiguration brings together these three stages.

51

The disciples are the chosen witnesses, following Christ on the path to suffering and glory so that what was written might be fulfilled. The Transfiguration was recorded in Matthew during the period of tension between the post-Easter period and that of End Time. Christ is risen but Christ will come again. The Church was affirming Jesus as Lord; he had fulfilled many of the prophecies about the Messiah in the Old Testament and the Church was awaiting his imminent return.

5. The Glory and the Exodus: the Gospel of Luke

The bringing of mankind to glory will be the prelude to the beginning of all creation. Is this hope mere fantasy? At its root there is the belief in the divine sovereignty of sacrificial love, a sovereignty made credible only by transfigured lives. (Michael Ramsey)[1]

We come now to the third, and most exciting, Gospel account of the Transfiguration. Luke weaves the Mark tradition neatly into his Gospel story along with some features of Matthew's story. He then adds some new material which is unique to this Gospel. Some understanding of the writer is important as we turn to a study of the Transfiguration in Luke. The Gospel of Luke and the Acts of the Apostles were written by the same person. Both works are dedicated to Theophilus. They have the same style and approach and the same enthusiasm for the subject of the Gospel being proclaimed to all people. But the author says very little about himself and we are left to glean elsewhere that Luke was a doctor of Gentile origin (Colossians 4:14). His Gentile background is crucial to our understanding of his Gospel and purpose. It is clear that he travelled with St Paul on some of his journeys (Book of Acts as evidence!) and that he was immersed in the life, witness and issues facing the first Christians. Luke's account of the Transfiguration is as follows:

Luke 9:28–36

(28) Now about eight days after this had been said, he took with him Peter, John and James and went up the mountain to pray.

(29) And it happened that, as he was praying, the aspect of his face was changed and his clothing became sparkling white. (30) And suddenly there were two men talking to him; they were Moses and Elijah appearing in glory, (31) and they were speaking of his passing which he was to accomplish in Jerusalem. (32) Peter and his companions were heavy with sleep but they woke up and saw his glory and the two men standing with him. (33) As these were leaving him, Peter said to Jesus, 'Master, it is wonderful for us to be here; so let us make three shelters, one for you, one for Moses and one for Elijah.' He did not know what he was saying. (34) As he was saying this, a cloud came and covered them with a shadow; and when they went into the cloud the disciples were afraid. (35) And a voice came from the cloud saying, 'This is my son, the Chosen One. Listen to him.' (36) And after the voice had spoken, Jesus was found alone. The disciples kept silence and, at that time, told no one what they had seen.

Michael Ramsey believed that Mark provides us with the most *historical* account of the Transfiguration, whilst Luke presents us with a *theological* assessment of the story by relating it to 'the inner life of Jesus'. There are three key differences of detail: Luke substitutes the verb 'to be transfigured' with the word *doxa* (glory), he also reveals that Jesus was talking about his *exodus*, which he was to accomplish in Jerusalem; throughout the scene Jesus is said to be *praying*. There are other less significant changes: there is a reference to 'eight' rather than 'six' days; a direct reference to Jesus' face being changed; the 'sleep' of the disciples and the association of fear at the coming of a cloud. These would suggest that Luke had access to a separate source as well as to the Gospel of Mark.

Riesenfeld is certain that Luke's purpose is very different from that of Mark; as a result the role of the disciples is diminished and there is a clear emphasis on three Greek words which are unique to Luke – praying, glory and exodus. Riesenfeld concludes that Luke is a paraphrase of Mark's text.[2] The notion of discipleship which emerges so clearly in Mark's account is also very strong in Luke. The same is true of Matthew's emphasis on Jesus fulfilling the Old Testament expectation of the Messiah. But there are clearly new dimensions and nuances to Luke's story which provide us with another explanation of the transfigured Lord on the holy mountain.

> **v. 28** Now about eight days after this had been said, he took with him Peter, John and James and went up the mountain to pray.

Luke is alone in using the number 'eight' to describe the days which passed between the Transfiguration and the preceding event. Both Mark and Matthew refer to six days. I. H. Marshall[3] suggests that Luke was probably influenced by Exodus 24:16 when he wrote of eight days: 'The glory of the Lord rested on Mount Sinai and the cloud covered it for six days. On the seventh day the Lord called to Moses from inside the cloud.' We cannot, however, be certain. It is more likely that all the evangelists simply want to express a period of time reflecting about a week. The Greek word for 'day' also has clear theological connotations. In the Old Testament the 'Day of the Lord' is often referred to and it has a variety of meanings. It could denote simply a day of joy (Amos 5:18; Zechariah 14:7) but in the later prophetic era it was also symbolic of the day of judgement and salvation (Joel 1:15; 2:2). In nearly all cases the 'Day of the Lord' is said to break into history in spectacular fashion. In later Judaism the idea of some future day of vindication and glory became an essential part of contemporary thought. The Messianic Age would be preceded by a time of chaos but the new age would be heralded by signs (Mark 13:23) and the 'end' (Mark 13:7) when the sinfulness of humanity would be overtaken by God's wrath, judgement and righteousness. Such a day was important to the Jewish community and it remains so today. I am convinced, however, that this was not the primary meaning of the word here.

Similarly, there are those who have tried to explain the Transfiguration as a misplaced resurrection account and they have stressed that the evangelists only really use the word 'days' when referring to the time that has elapsed since the resurrection. Delling[4] suggested that early Christian reference to the resurrection which mentioned the 'day' were influenced by Hosea 6:2: 'After two days he will revive us, on the third day he will raise us up and we shall live in his presence.' Bultmann's attempts to explain the Transfiguration as a misplaced resurrection account were helped by later Rabbinic writings where the resurrection of the Messiah was to take place 'after seven days'. But many other scholars have dismissed any connection between the Transfiguration and the resurrection simply on the basis of this time reference. There are several other allusions to the passing of days and time in the Gospels where there is no inference of any connection with the resurrection of Jesus (for example, Mark 1:32,35; 11:12,20; 14:1,12; 15:1).

As in Mark and Matthew, Jesus is accompanied by Peter, James and John when he climbs to the summit of the mountain. The parallel with Moses in Exodus 24:1,9 is obvious here and, whatever significance Luke saw in the revelation of Jesus' glory, the Old Testament understanding and background was of fundamental importance. The reference to Jesus going up into the mountain *to pray* is unique to Luke and is extremely interesting. Prayer is one of the great themes of St Luke's Gospel. It also plays a crucial role in the formation of the Early Church as recorded in the Acts of the Apostles. The author takes up references to prayer that already exist in Mark's Gospel and significantly adds to them. He suggests Jesus at prayer at special moments in his life and ministry, of which the Transfiguration is only one (cf. 3:21; 6:12; 9:18; 22:32). He also includes a great deal of teaching on prayer (6:28; 10:2; 11:1–13; 18:1–14; 21:36, 40,46). Prayer enables a Christian not to lose faith but to hold fast to that which is of God. In the period between now and the Second Coming Christians must pray to the Father who will reveal his purpose to them.

It is therefore no surprise that Luke has Jesus praying at his Transfiguration. Jesus is caught up in the presence of God as his glory is revealed. Michael Ramsey[5] already hints at a key phrase which he uses to interpret Luke's story: 'the transfiguration of suffering' is at the heart of Luke's understanding and the fact that Jesus is praying for help and guidance is obviously important.

v. 29 And it happened that, as he was praying, the aspect of his face was changed and his clothing became sparkling white.

The emphasis on prayer is repeated in this verse. The Transfiguration takes place as Jesus is praying. A visible change comes over his face and his clothes become sparkling white. There is an obvious link to the next verse where Luke confirms that this is all as a result of his glory being revealed. As we saw earlier, the description of Jesus is connected to both Old Testament and apocalyptic influences.

It is important to note here that, unlike Mark and Matthew, Luke fails to use the Greek verb 'to be transfigured'. This may be because the word 'transfigured' had a much wider use in Pagan circles. Both Ovid and Apuleius wrote works called *Metamorphoses* and in Hellenistic religions the word could also mean some form of religious transfiguration or conversion. It is also evident that the word played a role in Jewish Apocalyptic literature and it can be found in Daniel 12:3, 2 Baruch 51:3; Enoch 38:4; 104:2; 4 Ezra 7:97. Luke sticks with the Greek word *doxa*. As a result of the Transfiguration (this event is understood by the reader) the glory of God is revealed. To this extent Luke is more like the 2 Peter account.

v. 30 And suddenly there were two men talking to him; they were Moses and Elijah appearing in glory

This is a key verse in any study of the Transfiguration in the New Testament. The introduction of Moses and Elijah into Luke's story is overshadowed by his use of the Greek word *doxa*. The absence of the verb 'to transfigure' and the inclusion of this Greek word are key differences between Mark and Luke. Ironically, *doxa* is also used in the 2 Peter story where again it describes the glorious state into which Jesus was changed. If Peter was Mark's major source and the author of 2 Peter was using an authentic Peter source, it seems odd that Mark did not include the word also. But this has been explained simply by surmising that Mark preferred the more dramatic verb 'to be transfigured'.

In the Old Testament, a key Hebrew word is *kavod* (mentioned in Chapter 2), meaning a divine and heavenly state which is brought about by the presence of the glory of God. A full manifestation of the glory was expected to restore salvation to Israel (Psalm 96:3–9; Zechariah 2:5–11) at some time in the future. An understanding of the tension between past, present and future is necessary in any discussion about the meaning and significance of the glory of God. The concept of glory is important throughout the third Gospel. Even in the early chapters Luke refers to the glory sent from God for the people to see and respond to: 'An Angel of the Lord stood over them and the glory of the Lord shone round them.' (2:9); 'Glory to God in the highest heaven, and on earth peace for those he favours.' (2:14); 'A light of revelation for the Gentiles and the glory for your people Israel.' (2:32). Such references appear frequently in Luke where there is a continuous emphasis on the presence of the glory of God in Christ. That this glory was, at times, hidden from those who experienced it, seems obvious.

In the context of the Gospel of Luke, glory is linked inextricably to suffering. 'It is true that glory lay ahead for Christ, but it was a glory that could not be attained other than by way of suffering and death.'[6] Throughout the New Testament the link between glory and suffering is evident. Persecution and suffering were an integral part of Christian life in the Early Church and the link is firmly rooted there. In the opening chapter I suggested that St John did not include a narrative of the Transfiguration because he was concerned about the *gradual* manifestation of the glory of God in and through the person of Jesus. In most cases the *doxa* which is revealed in John points to a future, final revelation of God's glory in creation (John 1:14; 2:11; 7:18; 11:4; 11:40; 12:28; 17:4). But the passion of Jesus was part of the process whereby death could be defeated and glory finally revealed. It was an idea which St Paul clearly absorbed; he believed that Jesus would reveal the glory of God again at some time in the future. But the process of change and transfiguration was already happening: 'And all of us, with our unveiled faces like mirrors reflecting the glory of the Lord, are being transformed into the image that we reflect in brighter and brighter glory; this is the working of the Lord who is the Spirit.' (2 Corinthians 3:18).

When writing to the Romans Paul explains: 'So by our baptism into his death we were buried with him so that as Christ was raised from the dead by the Father's glorious power, we too should begin living a new life.' (Romans 6:4)

In other New Testament Letters, glory is seen as a characteristic of Jesus relating him directly to God (Romans 11:36; Galatians 1:5) through his suffering and resurrection; it was the presence of the glory of God which enabled Christ to overcome suffering.

> **v. 31** and they were speaking of his passing which he was to accomplish in Jerusalem.

Riesenfeld points out that Luke is the only evangelist to speak directly during the Transfiguration account about the passion which awaited Jesus. The Jerusalem Bible translates the Greek word *exodos* poorly; most other versions retain the direct, phonetic translation of *exodus* in English. Luke is certainly drawing a direct parallel between the forthcoming death of Jesus and the exodus of the people of Israel from Egypt. Just as the escape of Israel from the hands of Pharaoh meant the safe delivery of God's chosen people, so the death of Jesus in the holy city would lead to people being delivered from the sin that had imprisoned them.

Manek explains how the exodus became a way of understanding and interpreting history: 'The Exodus from Egypt was the basic fact of Israel's history. The revelation of God's intentions was given in the Exodus. The Exodus became a source of understanding history.'[7] He sees a direct and obvious link between the presence of Moses (and his act of deliverance) and the task awaiting Jesus in Jerusalem. The accent is firmly on the death of Jesus. The fact that Jerusalem is mentioned in this verse increases its importance as the place of Jesus' passion later in the Gospels. Marshall believes that it is from the moment of his Transfiguration, in the

Gospel of Luke, that Jerusalem becomes the goal of Jesus' ministry.[8] The road to Jerusalem would lead to death via the agony in the Garden. But the exodus obviously refers to the combined event of the death and resurrection of Jesus (Luke 9:51,53; 13:33ff.; 17:11; 18:31). To this extent we can translate *exodos* more as a deliverance than a death. What is certain is that Luke, more than any of the other writers of the Transfiguration story, highlights the connection between suffering and glory because of his use of *exodos*.

> **v. 32** Peter and his companions were heavy with sleep but they woke up and saw his glory and the two men standing with him.

Until this point in Luke's story, the disciples had experienced nothing. They were 'heavy with sleep'. The same verb is used in Mark 14:40 when the disciples are asleep in the Garden of Gethsemane. Luke may have used it here to emphasise their failure to understand fully what happened on the holy mountain until after the resurrection of Jesus. But the disciples do wake up and see exactly what is going on. They had missed the conversation about Jesus's exodus but they saw the glory revealed.

> **v. 33** As these were leaving him, Peter said to Jesus, 'Master, it is wonderful for us to be here; so let us make three shelters, one for you, one for Moses and one for Elijah.' He did not know what he was saying.

This verse is very similar to Mark's account except that here there is a reference to the early departure of Moses and Elijah. Luke may have added this to highlight the reason behind Peter's inane comment. Once again, what Peter says is irrelevant to what is happening on the mountain, but these words have assumed great significance as we reflect on the Transfiguration of Jesus today. 'It is good to be here.' How often do we say that when we wake up to a new morning, or when we arrive in church before a service begins? These words of St Peter on the mountain of the Transfiguration are worth reflecting on. We need to rediscover that sense of joy and privilege and expectation as we reflect on the love of God in our own lives. I shall have more to say about this in a later chapter. The rest of the background to this verse has already been discussed.

v. 34 As he was saying this, a cloud came and covered them with a shadow; and when they went into the cloud the disciples were afraid.

I have already briefly examined the role and function of the cloud in Judaism when I looked at Matthew's account. The cloud reminds us that God is present on the mountain. Though he is hidden from their eyes he makes his presence felt unequivocally. In Luke we are told that the cloud actually covers them – a reference perhaps to Exodus 40:34 where the cloud rests on the tabernacle which is filled with divine glory: 'The cloud then covered the Tent of Meeting and the glory of the Lord filled the Dwelling. Moses could not enter the Tent of Meeting, since the cloud stayed over it and the glory of the Lord filled the Dwelling.'

The verse in Luke is even closer to the following passage which appears in the Book of Exodus (24:15–18): 'Moses then went up the mountain. Cloud covered the mountain. The glory of the Lord rested on Mount Sinai and the cloud covered it for six days. On the seventh day the Lord called to Moses from inside the cloud. To the watching Israelites, the glory of the Lord looked like a devouring fire on the mountain top. Moses went right into the cloud and went on up the mountain. Moses stayed on the mountain for forty days and forty nights.' The glory and the cloud are the same here. When God is revealed his glory becomes visible. Moses goes into the cloud and is in communion with God. He speaks with him and shares with him, gaining guidance and strength for the future. At the Transfiguration Jesus, Moses and Elijah disappear into the cloud as the disciples look on. Some have questioned whether the disciples also entered the cloud but this seems unlikely.

v. 35 And a voice came from the cloud saying, 'This is my son, the Chosen One. Listen to him.'

The link between the voice of God at the baptism and the Transfiguration is, perhaps, most noticeable in Luke. The main difference is that at the baptism the voice conveyed a message to Jesus, whereas at the Transfiguration it is directed to the disciples. Jesus is emphatically declared the Son of God by the Father himself. But the link with the suffering servant figure of Isaiah is obvious here: this same baptised Son of God must also suffer and be put to death before he will be revealed in resurrection glory.

Various Old Testament passages suggest that the idea of the Son of God was one which had been around for a long time, for example, 'I will proclaim the decree of Yahweh; He said to me, 'You are my Son, today I have fathered you.' (Psalm 2:7). The title 'Son of God' emphasises the unique nature of the relationship between God the Father and Jesus the Son at the Transfiguration. It had a history both in Judaism and in the Gentile world. In the Old Testament the title is applied to kings, people with a special commission from God as well as to the Messiah. Oscar Cullmann concludes: 'the Old Testament and Jewish concept of the Son of God is essentially characterised, not by the gift of a particular power, nor by a substantial relationship with God by virtue of divine conception; but by the idea of election to participation in divine work through the execution of a particular commission, and by the idea of a strict obedience to the God who elects.'[9]

Many New Testament scholars understand the title 'Son of God' mainly in the contest of a suffering Christ. In many cases where the title is used there is at least a hint of suffering and sometimes the link is more obvious (Luke 4:3,9; Matthew 16:16; Mark 15:39). Cullmann adds: 'Jesus' consciousness of being the Son of God refers both to his person and to his work: his work of salvation and revelation shows that the Father and the Son are one. This conception of the Son of God is also the foundation of the faith of the first Christians, who in the light of the experience of Easter confessed him as the "Son".'[10]

> **v.36** And after the voice had spoken, Jesus was found alone. The disciples kept silence and, at that time, told no one what they had seen.

The theme of silence after the event is similar to that in Mark. Luke wishes to show that the disciples had to keep the experience to themselves and tell no one anything of what they had seen. Many scholars pinpoint two problems faced by Jesus' disciples: first, they did not always understand what was going on; and secondly, they were often told not to say anything to anyone about what had happened. This verse in Luke is a good example of what is sometimes called 'the Messianic Secret'. This command to silence was also given by Jesus after Peter had confessed him as Messiah at Caesarea Philippi: 'But he gave them strict orders and charged them not to say this to anyone' (9:21). Jesus teaches openly but he wishes that his identity should remain hidden for the moment.

The message of Luke

St Luke takes up the theme of discipleship which St Mark uses so powerfully and moves it on a step further. As I mentioned earlier, Bishop Ramsey made the point that Luke contains as much detail as Mark with a little more theology added for good measure. In emphasising the *doxa* of God, revealed in Christ who was at prayer and talking about his exodus to be accomplished in Jerusalem, Luke underlines some key points that help us to comprehend the depth and importance of this event in the life of Jesus. Marshall puts the emphasis on the future revelation of the glory of God: 'It was purely an experience for the Three, but one which is now recorded for all readers of the Gospel, so that they may have a foretaste of the heavenly glory of Jesus'.[11] The link between glory and suffering is the most vibrant theme of the Gospel of Luke. Even when the suffering seems to be unending – whether of body, mind or spirit – God is able to transform that suffering, as Michael Ramsey explains: 'Sometimes a person suffers greatly, and the suffering continues and does not disappear; but through nearness to Christ there is seen a courage, an outgoing love and sympathy, a power of prayer, a Christlikeness of a wonderful kind.'[12]

6. A Way of Understanding

There seems to be a certain dialogue of faith going on between the Father and the human race with Jesus in the centre. (Gerald O'Mahony)[1]

Theologians have battled with the biblical evidence of the Transfiguration for centuries. With so many key theological ideas in such a small passage, what is the Transfiguration really saying to the Church today? In the ministry of Jesus, what does the Transfiguration say to us about his teaching and our response to it? In what way is it connected with other key events in Jesus' life and mission? I will attempt here to explain the theological significance of the enigma of the Transfiguration.

Most of this chapter is dedicated to exploring the link between the glory of God that was revealed on the holy mountain and the glory that will be revealed when Jesus returns. The connection between the Transfiguration and the Second Coming pervades all theological discussion, but there are two other explanations which have gained wide respect over the years. Rudolph Bultmann clearly believed that the Transfiguration was a misplaced resurrection account which had been placed into the earthly life of Jesus. Harald Riesenfeld, however, examined the Old Testament background and understood the Transfiguration purely in terms of it fulfilling much of what was expected in the Jewish Cult as the Messiah was awaited. It was Boobyer who believed that the connection between the Transfiguration and the Second Coming held the key to our understanding of the event on the mountain.

A misplaced resurrection?

Bultmann insisted in the 1950s that 'the Transfiguration story, originally a resurrection account, dates his Messiahship from the resurrection onwards'.[2] Supporters of this view believe that some theologians have unfortunately succumbed to the temptation of abandoning the search for historicity in favour of analysing the theological meaning. They argue that if the disciples had truly witnessed the Transfiguration of Jesus, Peter would hardly have denied his Lord (Mark 14:66ff.; Matthew 26:69–75; Luke 22:56–62) and it is unlikely that the disciples would have reacted with so much fear after the crucifixion (Matthew 28:17; Luke 24:37). Others have dismissed this view altogether, claiming that the disciples' reaction throughout the Gospels is perfectly understandable regardless of what they had or had not seen beforehand. R. H. Stein believes that none of the theological motifs which we have just analysed in the Gospel accounts fits comfortably into a resurrection setting.[3] His most persuasive argument is his judgement that 'the glory of the Transfigured Jesus is a strong argument against, rather than for, the view that the Transfiguration is a misplaced resurrection account.'

Old Testament enthronement

Riesenfeld's book *Jésus Transfiguré*[4] has become a landmark in any study of the Transfiguration story. Scandinavian by birth, Riesenfeld chose to write his major study of the story in French. He believed that the Transfiguration of Jesus was, basically, a manifestation of Jesus' messianic glory in the course of his earthly life but that its theological significance was 'une problème évidemment insoluble au fond' (an insoluble problem). He highlights eight motifs and attempts to establish which principal theological ideas may have been behind the evangelist's portrayal of the transfigured Jesus.

Riesenfeld relies heavily on the Old Testament as he explores the motifs in detail – the mountain, the glory, the cloud, the voice, Moses and Elijah, the tabernacle, the rest and the passion. He explains the work of Mowinckel and other Old Testament scholars which established the existence of a clearly defined and organised Israelite Cult. His conclusion is very clear: the Transfiguration acts as the enthronement of Jesus as Messianic King in the same way that the Israelites celebrated the enthronement of God as King in the Old Testament. He believes that this would have been at the forefront of the evangelists' minds when they recorded the story and moulded it into their Gospels. The cloud and the voice denote God's presence; the mountain is the throne upon which the enthronement of Jesus as Christ the King will take place; Peter's suggestion to build three tabernacles is an attempt to enter into a perpetual rest to preserve Jesus as King. The whole of his argument depends on a presumption that the Israelite cult actually existed in the way that he suggests it did. Ziesler warned that his theory was entirely built on the presumption that there was such a thing as an Enthronement Festival but there is no proof that such an occasion ever took place.[5]

Parousia and glory

At this point I will return to the nature of the connection between the Transfiguration and the *parousia* (Second Coming). Throughout the examination of the Gospel evidence I made frequent reference to the relationship between the Transfiguration and the Second Coming of Jesus. Most scholars agree that, even if his overall thesis is not totally acceptable, Boobyer has, perhaps, the most relevant approach to finding a theological explanation for the Transfiguration story. A broad outline of Boobyer's work will help us to understand his approach and a little more about what the Second Coming meant to the Early Church.

Boobyer attempts to explain the original nature of the Transfiguration story at the beginning of his book. Each of the three explanations he offers contains certain Christological and historical presuppositions. His first suggestion is that the Transfiguration is a symbolic piece of writing which attempts to illustrate the messianic status of Jesus: 'it is unnecessary to suppose that any historical incident happened at all.'[6] Another interpretation is to regard the Transfiguration as a historical event but of a visionary nature. This would involve a close analysis of the presumption that, at the Transfiguration, it is the glory of God which is made visible either in a vision or in some other way. A third explanation is connected with the second in that he considers the possibility that the Transfiguration is a 'visionary forecast of the Resurrection of Jesus'. In simple terms, Boobyer suggests that rather than being a prefiguration of the *parousia*, the Transfiguration may well be a vision of the resurrected Jesus after his suffering is over but before the ascension and final vindication. He is, however, not content with such a theory and issues two warnings: (1) that when we are dealing with the thought of the Gospels, we must not speak of Christ's resurrection and exaltation as though they were two stages of one event; and (2) that we must not attribute to the evangelists a conception of Christ's resurrection body as a *doxa* body. Boobyer is convinced that there is no direct relationship between the Transfiguration and the resurrection.

In Chapter III Boobyer turns to the interpretation of the Transfiguration in the Early Church. This involves a consideration of 2 Peter and the Apocalypse of Peter. In my own examination of Mark's sources Boobyer's conclusions were important. He believes that there is a basic connection between the *parousia* and the Transfiguration and this is the general line he pursues for the rest of his book. He believes that there are four clearly defined areas of revelation within the life of the Early Church and to understand fully the Transfiguration of Jesus you have to comprehend these stages: pre-existence; hiddenness; revelation at the resurrection; revelation at the Second Coming. Boobyer is convinced that each of these periods is represented in the thought and writings of the Early Church and that we need to understand them clearly to comprehend the Transfiguration story.

'Pre-existence' suggests that the first Christians understood that Jesus was present with his Father from creation onwards – an idea which is strongly represented in the

67

Gospel of John and the Epistle to the Hebrews. It is not an idea which is apparent in Mark but Boobyer thinks it is implied: he points to Mark 1:1–13 and the use of the title *kurios* as being particularly important, as is the fact that Jesus is already called as the divine son of God by the voice from the cloud (1:11). Jesus is also ministered to by heavenly beings (Mark 1:13). Since Jesus proceeded from God, he was, therefore, in the beginning with God. The title 'Son of Man' adds weight to the notion that pre-existence is a characteristic of Mark's Jesus: in 2:10 Jesus has authority to forgive the sins of people because he is the Son of Man. Both the baptism and the Transfiguration stories in Mark's Gospel suggest that a pre-existent relationship between God and Christ was well established – that Jesus had been part of God's plan from the beginning.

The idea of 'hiddenness' or concealment is also important. The glory of the Transfiguration was revealed on the mountain after being concealed. It is arguably the most obvious stage in the process of Jesus' revelation in both the Epistles and the Gospels. Boobyer states that the first Christians believed that there was a period when the glory of God was temporarily concealed, when the glory voluntarily surrendered in becoming human flesh. Passages where such an idea is expressed are found frequently in the Epistles (for example, Galatians 24:4; Philippians 2:5ff.). Jesus disguised his true identity by coming in the flesh (Romans 8:3); though he was rich he was concealed as one who was poor (Corinthians 8:9) so that even the demons could not recognise him. The mystery of God's revelation was only now being made known to those who chose to receive this revelation (Colossians 1:25ff.). Throughout the Epistles there is the underlying suggestion that a period of concealment is not yet over and that after the resurrection there will be a time when Christ will be more fully revealed to mankind when he comes again (Romans 2:16; 1 Corinthians 4:5).

Hiddenness is an undeniably important aspect of the ministry of Jesus in Mark's Gospel. Jesus desires that his movements be concealed (1:35–38; 3:12,20; 4:31ff.; 7:17,24; 9:30) and he frequently obscures the precise meaning of his teaching (4:10–12, 34; 7:17; 8:27–31; 9:28). At times he does not clearly inform his disciples about his intentions (4:10,13; 4:40ff.; 6:49–52; 7:17ff.). There are also important instances where Jesus demands secrecy after healing someone (1:43ff.; 5:43; 7:36ff.) or where he commands his disciples (or even the demons!) not to say anything of what they have seen or heard (1:24ff.,34; 3:11ff; 8:30; 9:9). Scholars are divided as to whether or not the references to secrecy were an original part of the tradition that Mark received. Some suggest that the evangelist edited his sources in such a way as to introduce rather more examples of 'hiddenness' or 'secrecy' than there were in the original source. Boobyer's suggestion that the secrecy element in Mark represents 'the apostolic conception of the second stage of Christ's manifestation'[7] deserves serious consideration. To the Early Church (and no doubt to Mark also) the idea that Jesus' identity was in some way 'hidden' helped them to comprehend his dual identity as God and man. His hiddenness concealed his total oneness with the Father who had revealed him.

Just as the Kingdom of Heaven was hidden from the eyes of some people (Matthew 13:44) so the Son of God was also to be hidden from the eyes of many who failed to recognise his real identity. In the Gospel of Mark, Jesus remains hidden until his time has come and this seems to have been perfectly acceptable to the Early Church and to their concept of Christ according to the tradition handed on to them.

The other two stages in Boobyer's scheme are those of 'resurrection' and '*parousia*'. He suggests that the early Christians had a clear and precise definition of what they meant by the use of these terms and their theological significance. They were both events which, in the context of Jesus' earthly ministry, looked to the future. The resurrection was the revelation of Christ's real glory, whilst the *parousia* was a coming manifestation in complete splendour. The Early Church did not seem to regard the resurrection of Jesus as the complete unveiling of the concealed glory of Christ. At the resurrection, Jesus had triumphed over death (Colossians 2:15; 1 Corinthians 2:6–8) in what had

69

been a moment of great disclosure of the Messiahship of Jesus. The resurrection had also marked the beginning of a new age of salvation (1 Corinthians 10:11; 2 Corinthians 6:2) in which a day would come when the glory would be revealed to all those who had not seen the glory manifested when Jesus triumphed over death. Both the resurrection and the *parousia* are important stages in the process of revelation but they are not interchangeable events of equal significance.

In his analysis of Mark's Gospel, Boobyer looks at the relationship between resurrection and *parousia*. He believes that St Mark looks forward to some great day of future revelation. Material within Mark which can be regarded as futuristic can be placed into three broad categories:

1. Baptism in the Holy Spirit (Mark 1:8)
In the Apostolic era this would have been regarded as a sign of future revelation in light of the Easter events. The experience of Pentecost and the tradition of Jesus as one who could baptise in the Holy Spirit would have been significant.

2. Predictions of his passion and his own future (Mark 8:31; 9:31; 10:34)
These predictions look not only to Jesus' death but also to his resurrection and exaltation: 'they look beyond the cross to his subsequent triumph.'

3. Futuristic material of another kind (Mark 9:9; 10:37; 13; 14:25–28, 62)
Here, the resurrection and *parousia* are regarded as moments when the revelation process will move on a step further and the glory of God will be fully manifested now and in the future. In this context the Transfiguration of Jesus is recorded in both 2 Peter and the Gospels in the knowledge that the resurrection has already taken place and in anticipation of the Second Coming of Jesus at some future time.

I will now look more closely at the relationship between the Transfiguration and the Second Coming.

The Second Coming and the Transfiguration

In Advent 1993 the Bishop of Durham, Dr David Jenkins, said publicly that he doubted the existence of hell and was unsure about the Second Coming. Though his comments caused an uproar, they resulted once again in people talking about basic questions of salvation. Where does a life of discipleship lead us? Does hell exist? When and how will Jesus return to earth? The concept of a Second Coming in the life of the Early Church was uncertain and ambiguous. The link between the Transfiguration and the *parousia* can only be understood if we look closely at what evidence is available to us concerning the Second Coming.

There is no clear or obvious doctrine of the *parousia*. Uncertainty exists concerning the timing of the Second Coming, its effects, the nature of the final judgement, the manner in which God will glorify himself and how believers and non-believers will be dealt with. The expectation that the Messiah would return in the future at an undisclosed time was very much in evidence during Jesus' lifetime. But the imminence of the Messiah's return was indefinite and this caused confusion. Hanson writes: 'Indefinite imminence is a contradiction in terms . . . But though we may demythologise or transpose New Testament eschatology it is much too deeply engrained in the texture of New Testament thought for us simply to excise it without damage. Eschatological language was popular in Jewish writing. Apocalyptic literature, which strikes us as bizarre and grotesque, was in fact a familiar form of expression in Jewish circles from the second century BC to the second century AD. Eschatological interpretation of Jesus Christ was a Jewish way of emphasising his unlimited significance.'[8] The Second Epistle of Peter and the Synoptic Gospels must all be placed within this context. Jesus himself was understood (or misunderstood!) within this same context.

Frequently, during the course of his ministry, Jesus is

reported to have predicted that the Second Coming would take place very soon. There are numerous examples of this, including Mark 9:1; 13:38ff.; 14:62. I have already examined Mark 9.1 when I looked at the context of the Transfiguration in Mark. The warning here is that the Kingdom is coming. Norman Anderson suggests that Mark links 9:1 and 9:2–8 on purpose: 'Mark seems specifically to link it – as, presumably, a unique foretaste of the way in which the glory already inherent (although veiled) in Jesus would ultimately be fully revealed (2.Peter 1.16–18; cf 1.Peter 5.1).'[9] In his coming, the Kingdom of God had been proclaimed but the consummated Kingdom would appear at some future time.

The idea that God rules over earth and heaven is a central theme of the Old Testament. God's sovereignty was linked to the work of God in creation (for example, Psalm 104:5; 119:90; Isaiah 47:16; 1 Chronicles 29:11) through which his intention and plan for mankind and the created order were revealed. Similarly, in establishing a covenant between God and his people (for example, Exodus 19:5; Deuteronomy 14:2; 26:18; Psalm 135:4) the sovereignty of the Lord was made known in his dealings with mankind. But the failure of individuals to recognise the mighty power of God led to an increasing longing for God to demonstrate his authority and power at some time in the future. During the time of the Old Testament prophets, an expectation arose, despite the warnings of impending doom and destruction, that God would reveal himself finally and completely at some time in the future (Isaiah 44:6–23; Zechariah 14). Others believed that an intermediary figure would intervene on God's behalf – a Messiah (2 Samuel 7:12; Hosea 3:5), a Suffering Servant (Isaiah 42:1) or a Son of Man (Daniel 7). I will examine the importance of these titles with the Transfiguration story very much in mind.

The messianic figure of the Suffering Servant features prominently in that part of Isaiah which we call Deutero-Isaiah (chapters 40–55). There is no clear explanation as to who the Suffering Servant is, where he comes from or what his purpose is. His chief role seems to be one who was chosen by God in order to help his people as a mediator when the fullness of the glory of God was revealed at some future time. Parallels between the Suffering Servant and Jesus are obvious: it is in his suffering that Jesus accomplishes an essential stage in God's process of reconciliation between himself and the created order. In the Old Testament the Suffering Servant is a representative of the community of the people of God. A key passage here is Isaiah 42:1–3: 'Here is my servant whom I uphold, my chosen one in whom my soul delights. I have sent my spirit upon him, he will bring fair judgement to the nations. He does not cry out or raise his voice, his voice is not heard in the street; he does not break the crushed reed or snuff the faltering wick. Faithfully he presents fair judgement; he will not grow faint, he will not be crushed until he has established fair judgement on earth.'

This short passage, along with the more extensive account in Isaiah 53, are precise descriptions of the role of the Servant figure as he was understood in the prophetic era. In later Judaism, the Servant was directly associated with the expected messiah, although the relationship between the Servant and the Messiah titles is ambiguous and should not be over-simplified. This is also in evidence in the text of the Dead Sea Scrolls found at Qumran, where the Teacher of Righteousness assumes some of the characteristics of the Suffering Servant.

It is in the light of his own suffering that Jesus has been identified with the Suffering Servant figure and, as the Messiah, he brought these two titles and identities together within his own persona. The emphasis on the need for Jesus to suffer (for example, Mark 8:31; 9:31; 10:33) underlines his role as one who is prepared to suffer because of the folly of the world. The voice at his baptism (Mark 1:11) is a direct borrowing from Isaiah 42:1 and suggests that God addresses Jesus at his baptism in the same way as the servant is addressed at the beginning of the hymn in Isaiah 42. The link here with the Transfiguration is obvious and I will explore it shortly.

The title Son of Man is also important. It has its roots in the Old Testament but it assumed a new meaning during the life of Jesus. The most important reference in the Old Testament is undoubtedly Daniel 7:13: 'I was gazing into the visions of the night, when I saw, coming on the clouds of heaven, as it were a son of man.' Some have suggested that this is the beginning of a belief in a heavenly saviour-type figure who would be present at the End Time. T. W. Manson suggested that the Son of Man in Daniel was a corporate figure in the sense that he represented all those whom God had chosen by his redemption. Others disagree and suggest that the Son of Man was very much an individual figure. What is not clear is the relationship between the Son of Man and the Messiah. Both are distinct titles which came to be associated with each other mainly because of the ministry of Jesus. Writing about the various titles attributed to Jesus, Cullmann highlights the popularity of the title Son of Man: 'There are so many passages in the Synoptic Gospels in which Jesus definitely refers to himself as the Son of Man that we need not enumerate them all. Some scholars have asserted this title as a self designation of him, as an invention of the Evangelists based on the theology of the Early Church, but this all too simple thesis is disproved by the fact that Son of Man was not at all a common title for Jesus in the Early Church.'[10] It is obvious from the many examples that the title Son of Man did have eschatological overtones (for example, Luke 17:22ff.; Matthew 24; 27:37ff.; Mark 8:38). Son of Man and Suffering Servant are just two examples of figures referred to in Jewish literature who have been directly compared to the kind of figure who would play a key role on God's behalf at the end of time.

It is quite clear that the Early Church expected a quick return from Jesus. Many of its members were praying for this and some were waiting daily. Much of the apocalyptic imagery of the late-Jewish period was taken up and applied to Jesus the Messiah. They expected him to return and this time the glory would be permanent and the judgement would take place. It is clear that the Transfiguration was generally understood in this context in the Early Church: it was a glimpse of what God would do at the End Time.

7. Transfiguration Today

He lives again in the one who is truly given; the one who allows herself to live in His light, and to be made golden by the Sun of Love. (Elizabeth Ruth Obbard)[1]

How can we recapture the mystery and significance of the Transfiguration in our own hearts and lives today? To what extent can we encourage other Christians to bring the Transfiguration of Jesus back into the heart of the worshipping life of the Church, just as it was at the heart of Jesus' Galilean ministry? How, in this age with its need for evangelism and real communication of the words and works of Jesus, can his disciples be encouraged by the Transfiguration?

In the context of Jesus' earthly life there is no doubt that the Transfiguration was an extremely significant event. After his birth in Bethlehem and many years of preparation and contemplation in Nazareth, it was around the lakeside villages and towns of Galilee that Jesus proclaimed the Kingdom of God and called for repentance: 'The Kingdom of God is at hand. Repent and believe in the Gospel.' The religious leaders of his day could hardly believe what they heard and saw. Jesus seemed to have a unique authority, a special insight into the will of God. He preached in simple terms about profound truth. He healed the sick. He performed signs and wonders which no one else could explain. Word of him soon reached the southern hills of Israel and the capital city of Jerusalem. Those in the Temple did not believe that a carpenter's son from Nazareth could be the Messiah: it was impossible. When his Galilean ministry was almost complete Jesus began his final journey to Jerusalem.

75

He would weep over the City of David where he arrived as the Son of David; and he would be crucified on the outskirts of the same city as a common criminal. The resurrection would then show that Christ had defeated death and that the Kingdom of Heaven had begun.

As the bridge between Galilee and Jerusalem the Transfiguration sums up much of what Jesus represented as the central figure in religious history. The Transfiguration is both the climax and the close of his activity in the Galilee region and, in many ways, it is one of the greatest crises that Jesus faced during his time on earth. He had done what his Father had asked of him; he received divine affirmation; but the reality of suffering and rejection was only just beginning to dawn on him. To the disciples, the true significance of what took place would only fully make sense after the resurrection. But to Christians today, the Transfiguration story can be a source of help and strength to us in our daily lives.

True discipleship

First of all the Transfiguration teaches us a great deal about discipleship. Each of his disciples had responded to Jesus' call to 'follow me'. Their task was to share in the building up of the Kingdom of God (Luke 10:2). Jesus never pretended that the going would be easy and frequently talked in terms of complete sacrifice (Luke 9:57–62) and service (Luke 17:7–10). They were to 'travel light', to proclaim the coming of the Kingdom, to be hospitable and never to forget whom they represented. Jesus spent most of his earthly ministry teaching these twelve chosen men what God had instructed him to say. He gave them the Eucharist as an act of remembrance and taught them how to pray. The disciples were to be an example to others just as he was an example to them.

Throughout this study of the Transfiguration I have emphasised the role of Peter. He is the disciple with whom we can all identify. Peter, James and John were present with Jesus at times when the other disciples had been left behind. When they left the Transfiguration mountain the three would obviously have experienced a whole variety of feelings and emotions in response to what they had seen. These reactions would have been communicated at some time to the other disciples. This may have been shortly after the event or, as Wand suggests, after the resurrection: 'Strictly speaking we do not know what it could have meant at the time for the original twelve disciples as a body, because, according to the narrative itself, the very news of what had happened was deliberately withheld from the rest by the chosen three.'[2] Lewis Radford is certain though that the Transfiguration was crucial in the understanding of the Early Church on the question of discipleship: 'The Transfiguration of the Lord was a great formative experience for the three eye-witnesses. It was the climax of the training of their discipleship.'[3] The Transfiguration became an illustration to all disciples of Jesus through the centuries of the reality of discipleship and the Christian life. It offered basic clues and guidelines about what it means to follow Jesus. Discipleship involves sharing in eternal glory revealed in and through Jesus if we are prepared to suffer with him.

The mountain and the valley

You have to stand on Mount Tabor and imagine the Transfiguration yourself. The Sea of Galilee is only a few kilometres away. The hills of the various tribes of Israel and Judah can be seen as you survey the panoramic view. Jesus climbed to the summit of this high and lonely mountain with his three closest disciples and was transfigured before them. The fact that the change took place on a mountaintop is significant.

Of course, God reveals himself to us in many different ways, in a variety of places and through an assortment of people. But there are times in our lives when we need to withdraw, to be alone and to be only with God. If you think about it carefully, most of life is predictable. Many of our days, weeks and months are the same; life takes on its own routine. Only occasionally do we experience something which is extraordinary, out of the blue, exciting. We may witness a happening which stands out from the normal scenery of life and which changes or challenges us. But such high points are few and far between. Life as a whole is ordinary and commonplace, and so these special experiences touch us even more.

Church life can be very much like this. We go to church week by week without feeling anything out of the ordinary. Then we hear a piece of music, a Gospel passage, a prayer, or we hear a rousing sermon, attend a special service or see some stained glass or a painting which inspires us and encourages us in a new and invigorating way. In our own lives and relationships with others much of what we say and do is often repetition. But occasionally we have an experience that inspires and transforms us. We know that we cannot remain with that experience, that life must go on; like Jesus on the mountain, we know that we must come down and face whatever lies before us. And like Peter, James and John there are times when we, too, are full of wonder and perplexity. But the experience itself enhances our discipleship and encourages us to be more Christlike in all that we think and say and do. Bishop Ramsey writes: 'The scene on the mountain speaks to us today, but we are not allowed to linger there. We are bidden to journey on to Calvary and there learn of the darkness and desolation which are the cost of the glory.'[4] Mountaintops are not meant to be places where people live. They are places to visit, vantage points from which to enjoy the scenery, but then we must come back down to the valley.

In seeking to know God better great men and women of prayer frequently climb mountains that few of us could ever climb. And in doing so they help and encourage us. Austin Cooper, in his reflections on the writings of Mother Julian of Norwich, writes: 'The great men and women of prayer have climbed mountains most of us could never hope to scale and have discerned distant horizons most of us can hardly imagine. We do well to keep in mind the reality and validity of their vision of the things we are striving after. "They have caught some glimpse and hint of what no eye has seen or heard" (1 Corinthians 2:9).'[5]

78

Gladness

I have preached many sermons on St Peter's expression "Tis good, Lord, to be here'. If you are able to watch the recording of any television programme you will possibly be surprised by the many things that go on behind the scenes. Often, what you see on your television screen is a polished version of a whole series of different 'takes' and 'retakes' during which the producer and the director rely on the audience for a good deal of patience. But usually, before the recording begins, warm-up artists appear and try to invigorate the audience with some basic warmth and humour. The assembled crowd are told to look happy, to smile for the camera and to welcome the celebrity presenter with exuberance and joy. The outcome is the sight of a happy, excited audience which is pleased to be there.

I often think it would not be a bad idea to introduce this in our churches, up and down the country. One of the great disadvantages of being a priest is that you have to look at people's faces during worship! As an itinerant priest and preacher working throughout a diocese, I have been amazed to see how miserable and despondent people can be in church. It is commonplace to see people singing a joyful hymn with faces that say nothing of the love of God in which they can share; or to offer the peace to a congregation who give the impression that the heating was turned off three years ago! I often feel like shouting, 'Is it good to be here?' or 'Cheer up, for heaven's sake.' When certain religious programmes on television film worship in churches congregations have to be reminded to smile, to look happy, to look pleased to be there.

Peter's reaction – 'Tis good, Lord, to be here – is something that Christian disciples need to rediscover. The joy we can share daily in the love that God has given us in Christ is real; and we need to accept that joy and show it to others. It is true that the churches often attract people who have problems or who do not like smiling all the time. This is perfectly understandable. But to be in the presence of a loving and living God demands that we show a basic gladness

79

in our hearts and lives. Peter looked around him at the significance of the transfigured Christ; he recognised that on the Transfiguration mountain new hope was being offered to those who believed in Jesus as the Messiah. And he was happy to be there. He communicated that joy by saying the first (if not totally relevant) thing that came into his head.

In my own reflection on the Transfiguration of Jesus these words of Peter are constantly relevant and powerful. They are good words to wake up to. I remember one lady who had them typed out in large letters and placed above the bathroom mirror. Each morning when she brushed her teeth she reminded herself that this was a new day, a new beginning, and it was good to be alive! It is the same with worship, prayer and fellowship. However we might feel at certain times and in different places we need to take Peter's comments very seriously in our own time and place. Disciples of Jesus should daily mirror the joy of St Peter on the Transfiguration mountain and should be pleased that they can see and share in the glory which God revealed in Christ. St Anastasius, in a sermon on the Transfiguration, writes: 'Yes indeed, Peter, it is good for us to be here with Jesus and to remain here for ever. What is more blessed, what more sublime, what more exalted than to be with God, to be shaped into his likeness, to dwell in the light?'

Listening to God

So much has been written on listening in recent years that I can hardly do justice to such a major subject in this section. As disciples of Jesus on the mountain of the Transfiguration, Peter, James and John were told clearly by God to listen to what Jesus was saying: 'This is my beloved Son; Listen to Him.' The link with the baptism story has already been explored. Michael Ramsey points out that 'To hearken in biblical language means not just to listen to but listen and obey.'[6] God desired that the disciples should listen to and act on all the things Jesus had revealed and demanded of his followers. 'Here for a moment the disciples see the Messiah as rabbinic teaching pictured him, no longer the carpenter of Nazareth or even the well known teacher and healer, but the long-promised saviour of his people, in all the magnificence of a being who belonged as much to the other world as this. Such a witness to Peter's bold affirmation must have brought relief and comfort indeed.'[7] It was now a matter of faith and perseverance. Jesus had already talked a great deal. He had preached the coming of the Kingdom of God. He called people to repent of their past and to become his disciples. In word and in deed he encouraged them. Many local people listened to Jesus and responded with amazement, joy and faith. Others were not so sure. The religious leaders were, on the whole, furious at Jesus' ability to communicate so effectively with the majority of the people.

Noise is something that we have come to take for granted in today's world. I have lived both in the scenic setting of the Yorkshire Dales and (now) in the centre of London. Though both are markedly different, background noises of various sorts are in evidence throughout the day. Many of us are so uncomfortable at the prospect of silence that we immediately turn on the radio or television when we get up in the morning or come back home, not only for background noise, but as company. Very often we do not listen to what is being said but we are more comfortable with noise around us.

So how can God speak to us, how does the Father reveal his purpose and will to us in our daily lives? How can he transform us with his glory if we are not tuned in to what he is saying to us? We begin by recognising that God is indeed our heavenly Father. This is something we can so easily take for granted; it is something we need to recognise, accept and act upon. On the mountain of the Transfiguration the disciples saw not only a transfigured Son, they witnessed the voice of God and the Father's command to listen to Jesus. They were aware of God's presence with them. Thomas Merton explains that it is the Holy Spirit which directs us to see God as Father in order that, through Christ, we too can be transformed:

But our sonships before God is not a mere metaphor, or a legal

81

fiction. It is a supernatural reality. This reality is the work of the Holy Ghost who not only confers upon us certain rights in the eyes of God, but even heightens and perfects our personality to the point of identifying us, each individually, with the only begotten Son of God, Christ, the Incarnate Word . . . Each of us becomes completely himself when, in the Spirit of God, he is transformed in Christ.[8]

The Holy Spirit guides us today to recognise God as our heavenly Father. Having consciously prayed that we might be children of God, our task is to seek out the direction and purpose which God has ordained for us through Christ. This will always be a complex and often frustrating exercise. But learning to listen to what Jesus says to us remains a key spiritual challenge for many Christians today. Life becomes so cluttered; there is so much baggage.

For many clergy the command of God on the mountain of the Transfiguration is a dream rather than a reality. Many people, particularly those who are not connected with the Church, believe that clergy have a hot-line to God and are in daily touch with his will and purpose. But many full-time Christian workers find that the demands and, often, the loneliness of ministry means that they can so easily lose contact with God. I have been present at many church meetings, gatherings and events where I have had to remind myself of the need for prayer, reflection and God-centredness. 'Listen to him' is a divine command which many in the ordained ministry would like more time and space to carry out. Church politics and other issues can so easily get in the way. In our leading of worship, intercessions, preaching and visiting we can all develop that gift of listening to what Jesus would say to us. This enhances our discipleship.

The Church in the nation often gives the impression that it has cut off lines of contact with its heavenly Father. After many years as a press officer in the Church of England I frequently sit back and reflect on the Transfiguration: why don't we learn to listen again to the voice of God in Christ? If you sit in the public gallery at any meeting of the General Synod of the Church of England you will notice that there is a tremendous amount of talking and listening, one member to another, but not a great deal of time and space given to obeying the divine command of God on the summit of the Transfiguration mountain. Clergy and laity both need to reflect on this divine command to listen to Christ. The same is true of each and every baptised believer. The need to spend some time in quiet reflection or meditation each day is a basic and important one. To listen to Christ is to be in tune with God; to be in tune with God is to be guided and strengthened by the Holy Spirit. That can be our daily mountaintop experience if we put the world to one side and listen to him.

The Transfiguration is indeed concerned with the nature of discipleship. The event reminds us that life is often predictable but that, occasionally, we will have mountaintop experiences which will transform us and challenge us. Peter points to the joy of serving Christ who is our Lord and Saviour. And the divine voice is also a reminder that we need to listen to what Christ is saying. As we go about the task of mission as disciples of Jesus, these basic insights, offered to us by the Transfiguration, enable us to be more effective and to share that good news with others.

8. A Glimpse of the Mystery

Heaven and earth meet, the temporal meets the eternal, the human is transformed into the divine. (A. R. C. Leany)[1]

The key to true discipleship in the New Testament is the acceptance of the inevitability of Jesus' suffering and the conscious decision of the believer to identify and share in it. There can be no resurrection, no glory, without suffering first. The Transfiguration provides us with a graphic account of how God transforms the suffering of the world in the person of Christ. It can help us understand some of those things which seem incomprehensible in our daily lives, whether at an individual or a corporate level.

Predictions

The inevitability of Jesus' suffering is established in St Mark's Gospel immediately after Caesarea Philippi and the Transfiguration narrative. In many respects Peter's confession at Caesarea acts as a trigger that makes Jesus realise the inevitability of the suffering that lies ahead of him:

> Then he began to teach them that the Son of Man was destined to suffer grievously, and to be rejected by the elders and the chief priests and the scribes and to be put to death and after three days to rise again; and he said all this quite openly. Then, taking him aside, Peter tried to rebuke him. But turning and seeing his disciples he rebuked Peter and said to him, 'Get behind me Satan! You are thinking not as God thinks, but as human beings do.' (Mark 8:31–33)

This is one of three predictions of Jesus' passion made by Our Lord in the final weeks of his ministry (cf. 9:31; 10:33ff.). They are general statements about the nature of Jesus' ultimate fate but they have a direct bearing on what will take place in Jerusalem. It is likely that the disciples were frightened by Jesus' predictions of his suffering; certainly it seems that they did not understand this aspect of his mission at this stage and it is something that they were anxious to forget. To this extent Jesus knew real loneliness. He understood his fate clearly after Caesarea Philippi but the disciples remained somehow detached and often confused until after the crucifixion.

I have already stressed the importance of Isaiah 53 in any discussion about suffering in the New Testament. In much of Jesus' own understanding of his passion there is an underlying acceptance of what he must endure: a sense of service in suffering, the Suffering Servant, which is a central theme in Isaiah 53. Hunter explains: 'If we are to understand how Jesus conceived of his passion, we must begin with Isa. 53. And the doctrine of that chapter is one of representative and redemptive suffering for others, with the idea of substitution well in the foreground (see Isa. 53.4–6).'[2]

Immediately after the Transfiguration Jesus again refers to the need for him to suffer. It becomes part and parcel of his very being as his eyes are fixed on Jerusalem. He is fully aware of the extent of the sinfulness of mankind and sets his will resolutely towards Jerusalem. *Part of the cost of discipleship is an awareness of the need to suffer.*

Prayer

In St Luke's account of the Transfiguration Jesus is praying when the light shines on his face. Ramsey reminds us: 'We do not know that it is a prayer of agony and conflict like the prayer in Gethsemane, but we do know that it is a prayer near to the radiance of God and the prayer of one who has chosen the way of death.'[3] We do not know what Jesus prayed and we rely only on St Luke's account for evidence here. But most scholars believe that the prayer of Jesus on the

Transfiguration mountain was connected in some way with the inevitability of the suffering that lay ahead. As Radford suggests, 'It was probably prompted and shaped by the thought of the Passion which He had so recently predicted, and perhaps only recently foreseen for the first time.'[4]

The connection between prayer and suffering is focused on strongly in the events on the top of the mountain. In *Glimpses of the Divine*,[5] Bishop Bulley wrote: 'It is good to seek moments of "transfiguration" – in a retreat, in Sunday worship, in our prayers – but from the mountain of glory we have to descend to the plain – of work, of pain maybe, of difficulties, of problems, of suffering. That we can do with confidence that the glory will shine through for us as it did for the apostles.' We can all identify with this. A regular discipline of prayer and devotions always results in high and low points – times when we feel we are in communion and are communicating with our Father and other times when we seem to be lost and uncertain. Austin Cooper, in his book on Julian of Norwich, writes: 'We need to pray for the grace to catch some glimpse of the mystery of transfiguration.'[6]

Exodus

Once again, St Luke is the evangelist who clarifies what Jesus, Moses and Elijah were talking about and in my brief look at the Luke story I asked some basic questions about his use of the word 'exodus'. Hooke suggested that with the Transfiguration 'we have reached the point where the final exodus is to take place.'[7] Simply to translate this word as 'death' would be incorrect. Some have suggested that Jesus' thought must have been mainly on the prediction of future events in Jerusalem which he had made a few days before at Caesarea Philippi, but the word exodus seems to have a more dramatic meaning here. Luke is referring to the whole of Jesus' saving acts: his death, resurrection and glorious ascension.

That is not to say that Luke lost sight of what Jesus would have to endure. The human suffering of Jesus is conveyed very powerfully in all four Gospels. But it is because of the Transfiguration story happening when and where it did that there is already hope for those who have faith in Jesus Christ. The exodus would mean deliverance as it had in the past. But there could be no freedom from bondage – no release from sinfulness – in dealing with the extent of the suffering first. As we read of Jesus, Moses and Elijah discussing his exodus, it is possible to imagine these two great Old Testament figures encouraging Jesus, the Son of God, to transform and change a situation which for them had always pointed forward to the coming of a Messiah.

Jesus was aware of the need for suffering but he was confident that the same Father who had affirmed him at his baptism would deliver him from sin and death, raise him to new life and perfect the glory which was now temporarily revealed, once and for all.

The transfiguration of suffering

In the next chapter I will examine the implications for us today of the glory which was revealed on the mountaintop. How can we share in that glory which was embodied in Jesus? A first step here is a faith that accepts the ability of Jesus to transform the suffering which is an inherent part of our daily lives as Christians. Suffering is a theme that occurs in many biblical books. Personal suffering is evident in many of the Psalms (for example, Psalm 22) and in the Book of Job. But the idea of vicarious suffering finds its true home in Isaiah 53. The experiences of the Suffering Servant are seen to be as a result of the sinfulness of the people (53:4–6).

The suffering of Jesus needs to be seen in the history of the Jewish tradition into which he was born. Through his suffering Jesus learnt obedience (Hebrews 5:8) and we are now expected to share in the suffering. In Romans 8:35, 37, St Paul points us in the right direction: 'Can anything cut us off from the love of Christ – can hardships or distress, or persecution, or lack of food and clothing, or threats or violence; No, we come through all these things triumphantly victorious by the power of him who loved us.' Paul never pretends that life is easy. He is always keen to earth the Christian life in reality. But he is equally certain that no amount of suffering, testing or hardship should be able to separate us from the love of God: and he uses the Greek word *dunamis* which is in the 2 Peter account of the Transfiguration to underline his point. It is in and through the power of God that the suffering of the world is transformed and changed.

As a priest I can think of many situations where the faith of individuals or small groups of people has transformed a potentially tragic or painful situation into one where faith has clearly helped them and others. It may be someone facing certain death but who for the moment is conscious, active and wholesome in their approach to life. The breakdown of relationships always results in the need for healing, faith and perseverance in the face of rejection, hopelessness and despair. Unemployment, financial problems, drug addiction, homelessness: the list of problems which can affect us is endless, but Christ is able to transform whatever challenges we face.

Michael Ramsey's understanding of the Transfiguration is rooted in the idea that true discipleship demands an acceptance of suffering. The chapter 'The Mount and the Plain', in his book *Be Still and Know*, is a classic in its own right on the theme of the transfiguration of suffering: 'Transfiguration is indeed a central theme of Christianity, the transforming of sufferings and circumstances, of men and women with the vision of Christ before them and the Holy Spirit within them.' He believes that the transfiguration of suffering is well attested in the Christian life. Circumstances are transfigured. Problems and issues which affect us are not ignored or removed but are lifted with Christ on to the cross at Calvary. Ramsey adds: 'We are bidden to journey on to Calvary and there learn of the darkness and desolation which are the cost of the glory.'

To suffer as a baptised believer of the Church is to suffer with Christ. And we accept the suffering that is in the world in the context of the Kingdom of God being revealed on earth. A Christian asks God to transfigure the suffering and to lead him to the glory of the transfigured Jesus. Sister Sheila Margaret, C.S.M.V., wrote a beautiful poem called 'Transfiguration',[8] reproduced below, which encapsulates the sense of suffering being transformed.

> Think not to roam at will the distant hill
> And drink the heady wine of morning air,
> To linger long beside some sparkling rill
> Amidst the marshy, flower-strewn meadows there.
> These things in surfeit tend to be but loss
> For we are nailed to life as to the cross.
>
> Long may our sojourn be upon this plain,
> And dim the way our feeble footsteps tread,
> While all our strivings seem to be but vain
> And heart is weary, inspiration dead.
> Yet in the furnace, gold is purged of dross
> And Christ has triumphed for us on the cross.
>
> So lift up your heart to Christ upon the mount,
> Drink deep to fill its emptiness again.
> He fills us all, turns all to good account,
> For he descends the footpath to the plain
> To heal the leper, making whole the loss,
> Before he nails us with him to the cross.

9. Glory Be to Jesus

Ad majorem Dei gloriam
To the Greater Glory of God

The glory of God was revealed on the mountain and the disciples beheld his glory. The presence of glory was the main evidence for Jesus' Transfiguration. It gave confidence and delight to those who witnessed it. But the glorious scene was a temporary one and the road to suffering and the holy city had to be travelled first. For Calvin the Transfiguration was 'a temporary exhibition of his glory'. It was visible for a short period to remind the disciples of the need for faith. There could be no glory without suffering for Jesus and for his disciples. It is important that we think about exactly what this glory means for us today. St Paul tells us that we can share in the Transfiguration glory if we are prepared to be changed and to transform our own lives (2 Corinthians 3:18). St John believes that this glory was present in the beginning with God, made itself visible in the life and ministry of Jesus, and will be present when Christ returns (John 1:1–14). If we are prepared to take up our cross and follow Jesus on the path of discipleship, we will be able to understand and share more fully in the divine glory.

The concept of the glory of God figures prominently in the Old Testament. The Hebrew word *kavod* – the reigning glory of God – is constantly being revealed. It is most used alongside verbs of seeing (Exodus 16:7) and appearing (Isaiah 60:1). The Hebrew tabernacle was to be the centre of the revelation of the glory of God to the people (Exodus 45:34ff.). In the Psalms the glory of God enters through the gates of the Temple (Psalm 24:7ff.). The *kavod* was expected to be a fundamental sign of the Messiah when he came. The glory revealed by the Messiah would be unique; it would restore the glory originally lost by Adam. The purpose of the *kavod* at the end of time was salvation to Israel (Isaiah 60:1): 'Arise, shine out, for your light has come, and the glory of the Lord has risen on you.' It would convert other nations who could not see the love of God (Psalm 96:3–9).

In the period immediately preceding Jesus' coming, the idea of the glory being perfectly restored after the fall of Adam gained new importance. In many Jewish apocalyptic writings the Rabbis described salvation as a vision of the glory of God. As Hoskyns rightly points out, 'the manifestation of the glory of God is, however, in the Old Testament still incomplete. The hope for the future was that the glory of God would be exalted above all the earth, that all nations would see his glory and that he would deliver his beloved by a great act of judgement.'[1]

The Greek word *doxa* which St Luke uses in his Transfiguration story can be found 165 times in the New Testament. As we saw in an earlier chapter when I examined his account, sometimes it is used to represent 'honour' or 'fame' but many of the references are as a direct result of the Old Testament understanding mentioned above. God is variously described as the God of glory (Acts 7:2), the Father of glory (Ephesians 1:17) and the majestic glory (2 Peter 1:17). God is frequently said to be a glorious God and the verb is also used of Christ himself (Luke 9:32; John 1:14; 1 Corinthians 2:8). But throughout the New Testament there is a definite emphasis on a futuristic yearning for the divine glory to be finally, completely and totally revealed – once and for all. This is, of course, part of the yearning of the Early Church for the Second Coming of Jesus to arrive quickly. The glory would be an essential aspect of the glorious return of Jesus (Romans 8:18; Colossians 3:4). In the meantime, however, the glory helps us and sustains us in a world of suffering and sin.

Michael Ramsey frequently explains that Luke first tells us how the glory of God is made visible in the story of the birth and ministry of Our Lord. Ruth Burrows also points to the song of the angels at the birth of Jesus: 'And suddenly there was with the angel a multitude of the heavenly hosts praising God and saying Glory to God in the highest, and on earth peace to men who are God's friends.'[2] This is a reminder that the glory of God which we read about so much in the Old Testament was present even with the infant Jesus. Burrows writes: 'This is God's glory, glory in the highest – that He should communicate Himself fully to the lowest; that each of us should receive to our full capacity the love He longs to bestow. It is possible now because of this little Child.'[3]

In the doxology we say: 'Glory be to the Father and to the Son and to the Holy Spirit; as it was in the beginning is now and ever shall be, world without end, Amen.' This glory revealed to us in the past is now being revealed in the transfigured Jesus, and will be more fully revealed in the future at the Second Coming of Christ. To understand the glory in the Transfiguration properly we must see this interaction of glory in the past, present and future.

Christ, the second Adam, restores that glory to creation. The *doxa* is fully absorbed and made perfect in the transfigured Jesus when we see a glimpse of the glory that will be revealed once the suffering has been endured. The dynamic relationship between Father and Son is shown in the Transfiguration glory. Marshall points out: 'It is true that the glory lay ahead for Christ but it was a glory that could not be attained other than by way of suffering and death.'[4]

St John

The fact that St John fails to mention the Transfiguration in the fourth Gospel does not mean that he is not interested in the idea of the glory of God or the Transfiguration story: on the contrary! In his famous Prologue, John writes: 'The word became flesh, he lived among us, and we saw his glory, the glory that he has from the Father as only Son of the Father, full of grace and truth.' (1:14) The faith of the Church rests on the fact that 'we saw his glory'. Eyewitnesses of the divine glory believed that Christ offered new hope and new life to the world. Barrett believes that this verse shows why John may feel that there is no need to include the Transfiguration in his Gospel as a story: 'The Transfiguration is not recorded in John, and of the agony in Gethsemane there remain only traces in 12.27–30; 18.11. Here perhaps most clearly of all we see how Marcan incidents have been developed by John into major themes of his Gospel. Throughout the gospel run the twin themes of the glory of Jesus, manifested not once only on the holy mountain but – for those who had eyes to see – continually throughout his incarnate life, and of his obedience to his Father's will, even in humiliation and suffering (cf eg 4.34). It is a definition of Jesus as described in John that he is at once glorious and humiliated.'[5]

The glory is present throughout the Gospel of John. At Cana in Galilee Jesus performs his first miracle when he turns the water into wine: 'This was the first of Jesus' signs: . . . He revealed his glory and his disciples believed in Him.' (2:11). At Bethany, on the outskirts of Jerusalem, Jesus raises Lazarus from the dead and he says: 'This sickness will not end in death, but it is for God's glory so that through it the Son of God may be glorified.' (11:4). The glory that Jesus revealed dated back much further than the Incarnation. 'Now Father, glorify me with that glory I had with you before ever the world existed.' (17:5). The glory was with Jesus when he was present with the Father in creation. Jesus is always seen as being completely obedient to the Father's wish and John begins to use the word 'glorified' to describe the death of Jesus: 'He was speaking of the Spirit which those who believed in him were to receive; for there was no Spirit as yet because Jesus had not yet been glorified.' (7:39), and 'At first his disciples did not understand this, but later, after Jesus had been glorified, they remembered that this had been written about him and this is what had happened to him.' (12:16). Throughout the Gospel of John there is a specific link between the death of Jesus and his glorification.

This helps us to understand the Transfiguration narrative

in the Synoptic Gospels more clearly. It reinforces my argument in the previous chapter that discipleship is inextricably linked with suffering. Jesus' uniqueness is his Sonship. It is because he is the Son of God that glory is revealed through him and in him. So when, in 1:14, John talks about Jesus as 'only Son of the Father' a connection between the Transfiguration and the baptism story emerges. In Mark's account of Jesus' baptism, God declares: 'You are my Son, the Beloved; my favour rests on you' (1:11). What is very interesting is that St John ignores this detail in much the same way as he avoids a direct reference to the Transfiguration. John explains throughout his Gospel that the glory of God was revealed in the person of Jesus because Christ is God's only Son, incarnate with him in the beginning. In our own baptism we become sons and daughters of God through adoption, as the Anglican Service makes clear: 'Lord God our Father, maker of heaven and earth, we thank you that by your Holy Spirit these children have been born again into new life, adopted for your own, and received into the fellowship of your Church: grant that they may grow in the faith into which they have been baptised, that they may profess it for themselves when they come to be confirmed, and that all things belonging to the Spirit may love and grow in them.' (ASB Baptism Service)

This prayer of reception and welcome would be appreciated by St John the Evangelist. It is because we are children of God through our own baptism that we can now be transformed and changed into his likeness. It is because God is our Father that we can attempt to walk in faith with him. A decision to be obedient to God, to accept his will, to walk in his way, is made in baptism. But, as St Paul reminds us time and time again, this path of discipleship is a lifelong commitment of faith and trust in God.

The challenge of St Paul

St Paul writes in 2 Corinthians 3:18: 'And all of us, with our unveiled faces like mirrors reflecting the glory of the Lord are being transformed into the image that we reflect in

94

brighter and brighter glory; this is the working of the Lord who is the Spirit.' The only time St Paul uses the Greek verb 'to transfigure' is when he is trying to explain how we can share in the glory of God as it is revealed in Christ. In many ways his teaching is complementary to that of St John. On the mountain of the Transfiguration Jesus is recognised, accepted and loved as the Son of the Father. In the same way, those who have faith in a loving and living God will be recognised, accepted and loved by him. Cooper writes: 'Our Lord's Transfiguration is not a remote event or a contrived poetic image. It is the meaning of our human growth and our destiny – glory.'[6]

But personal transfiguration from a life of doubt and atheism to a life of faith and light is not a once-and-for-all event. On the mountain we see a glimpse of the glory which had been present since the creation. But it soon disappeared as the reality of Jerusalem loomed ahead. This is what the disciples failed to understand at the time. It only made perfect sense after the Ascension of Jesus into heaven. Throughout his Letters Paul always emphasises that the Christian life is a process, a journey, a pilgrimage. Though he was converted to Christianity on the road to Damascus by the light of God, he stresses that it is not a question of everything being achieved at once.

From the moment of our baptism we become children of God and a process of transformation begins. Paul uses words like 'new birth', creation, grafting, nourishment to explain this process. In 2 Corinthians 3:18, he suggests that with the guidance of the Holy Spirit we are being transformed daily into what God wants us to be. Christ has given us a way ahead – hope for the future – but the glory necessarily involves suffering first until the Second Coming finally takes place.

'The mystery of the Transfiguration challenges us to hold in some tension the reality of the present moment and the reality of the call to glory' writes Cooper.[7] We do this in our daily lives as Christian people, in our reading of the Scriptures, our daily prayers and devotions, in our actions, words and thoughts. Bishop Wand, a former Bishop of London,

sums this up perfectly: 'The process of transfiguration con-
sists in the gradual change by which this new man assumes
larger and larger proportions of the individual personality.
The process is assisted by the continual influence of the
Holy Spirit and by repeated participation in the Eucharist.'[8]
We sing the *Gloria in Excelsis* in the service of Holy Communion fully aware of the tension in which we live as sinners
and yet as baptised children of God:

> Glory to God in the highest,
> and peace to his people on earth.
> Lord god, heavenly King,
> almighty God and Father,
> we worship you, we give you thanks,
> we praise you for your glory.
> Lord Jesus Christ, only Son of the Father,
> Lord God, Lamb of God,
> You take away the sin of the world:
> have mercy on us;
> you are seated at the right hand of the Father:
> receive our prayer.
> For you alone are the Holy One,
> you alone are the Lord,
> you alone are the Most High,
> Jesus Christ,
> with the Holy Spirit,
> in the glory of God the Father. Amen.

And as we share in the bread and wine we are aware that it
is the glory of God which sustains and upholds us; it is that
to which we look for strength and reassurance.

Gerald O'Mahony sj in a series of prayers and meditations
on the Gospel of Mark thinks of his own confirmation when-
ever he reads the Transfiguration story. 'On the day I was
confirmed, the Church celebrated my transfiguration . . .
Anyone can admit to being God's child when life is going
smoothly. To acknowledge him as Father when everything
goes wrong takes a power we do not possess from ourselves.
Yet God does not call without giving us the power to answer

the call, if we think but ask for it earnestly. I picture the day of my confirmation, the day I was called to witness to my faith. I imagine myself at the scene of the transfiguration. I bring the two together and reflect that I too was transfigured on the day that I was confirmed.'[9]

The Transfiguration of Jesus took place at a crucial moment in Our Lord's life. It confirmed God's vindication of him as Son of God and Peter's claim that in Jesus the expected Messiah had come. Later Peter, James and John revealed the significance of the story to the first Christians. A part of the Peter tradition is preserved in 2 Peter; Mark, Matthew and Luke all built on that source and used their own information and material. St John, whilst ignoring the story directly, believed that the same transfiguration glory was continually being revealed throughout Jesus' life, death and resurrection. As the Early Church grew there was a clear desire to understand the Transfiguration in the light of the expected return of Jesus.

Even in this brief summary of the Transfiguration in the New Testament it is possible to see how and why Christians through the ages have found it a difficult story to wrestle with in their own lives and worship. Though it really is undiscovered treasure, many tend to let the story rest where it is and to remain an enigma. The story is full of Old Testament imagery: it shows Jesus as the fulfiller of the Old Covenant. It points forward to a final scene of glory and fulfilment yet to be witnessed. But most important of all, it speaks to us now.

Fr O'Mahony speaks of his own transfiguration. All of us are aware of aspects of our lives which we want to see changed and transformed. St Paul is right to emphasise the point that even in our baptism that transfiguration is already underway. Now it is a question of faith and trust that the suffering which will affect our paths as disciples will be completely and finally transfigured by the same God of Glory who vindicated Jesus. Our task is to listen to God; to be changed from glory to glory; to seek guidance and strength from this wondrous scene on the mountain where eternal glory gives hope to the human race.

Epilogue
Prayers and Devotions: an Office of the Transfiguration

This office is adapted from a similar one provided in Lewis Radford's small book on the Transfiguration[1] and is of great help at any time when we wish to reflect on the Transfiguration of Jesus.

The Invocation and the Lord's Prayer may be said silently. The Reader shall begin the Office.

V: With you, O Lord, is the well of life.
R: And in your light shall we see light.
V: Send out your light and your truth that they may lead me.
R: And bring me to your holy mountain and to your dwelling.

All standing, the Reader shall continue:

V: Glory be to the Father, and to the Son: and to the Holy Spirit;
R: As it was in the beginning, is now, and ever shall be; world without end. Amen.

Hymn

Be still, for the Spirit of the Lord, the Holy One, is here.
Come, bow before Him now, with reverence and fear.
In Him no sin is found, we stand on holy ground.
Be still, for the Spirit of the Lord, the Holy One is here.

Be still, for the glory of the Lord is shining all around;
He burns with holy fire, with splendour He is crowned.
How awesome is the sight, our radiant King of light!
Be still, for the glory of the Lord is shining all around.

Be still, for the power of the Lord is moving in this place,
He comes to cleanse and heal, to minister His grace.
No work too hard for Him, in faith receive from Him;
Be still, for the power of the Lord is moving in this place.[2]

Then the Reader shall begin the Antiphon:

Antiphon   We shall be like him; for we shall see him even
as he is. (1 John 3:2)

Then the following Psalms shall be read or sung:

Psalm 2

1. Why this uproar among the nations, this impotent muttering of the peoples?
2. Kings of the earth take up position, princes plot together against the Lord and his anointed,
3. 'Now let us break their fetters! Now let us throw off their bonds!'
4. He who is enthroned in the heavens laughs, the Lord makes a mockery of them,
5. Then in his anger rebukes them, in his rage he strikes them with terror.
6. 'I myself have anointed my king on Zion my holy mountain.'
7. I will proclaim the decree to Yahweh: He said to me, 'You are my son, today I have fathered you.
8. Ask of me and I shall give you the nations as your birthright, the whole world as your possession.
9. With an iron sceptre I will break them, shatter them like so many pots.'
10. So now, you kings, come to your senses, you earthly rulers, learn your lesson!

11. In fear, be submissive to Yahweh;
12. With trembling, kiss his feet, lest he be angry and your way come to nothing, for his fury flares up in a moment. How blessed are those who take refuge in Him!

Glory be to the Father and to the Son and to the Holy Spirit; as it was in the beginning is now and ever shall be, world without end. Amen.

Psalm 99

1. Yahweh is king, the peoples tremble; he is enthroned on the winged creatures, the earth shivers;
2. Yahweh is great in Zion. He is supreme over all nations;
3. Let them praise your name, great and awesome; holy is he and mighty!
4. You are a King who loves justice, You establish honesty, justice and uprightness; in Jacob it is you who are active.
5. Exalt Yahweh our God, Bow down to his footstool; holy is he!
6. Moses and Aaron are among his priests, and Samuel, calling on his name; they call on Yahweh and he answered them.
7. He spoke with them in the pillar of fire, They obeyed his decrees, the Law he gave them.
8. Yahweh our God, you answered them. You were a God of forgiveness to them, but punished them for their sins.
9. Exalt Yahweh our God, bow down at his holy mountain; holy is Yahweh our God!

Glory be to the Father and to the Son and to the Holy Spirit. As it was in the beginning is now and ever shall be, world without end. Amen.

Then the Antiphon shall be said by all together:

Antiphon   We know that, when he shall appear, we shall be like him; for we shall see him even as he is. (1 John 3:2)

Reading
He was still speaking when suddenly a bright cloud covered them with shadow and suddenly from the cloud there came a voice which said, 'This is my Son, the Beloved; he enjoys my favour. Listen to him.' (Matthew 17:5)

R: Thanks be to God.

V: We all are being transformed into the same image, from glory to glory, even as from the Lord the Spirit. (2 Corinthians 3:18)

R: We all are being transformed into the same image, from glory to glory, even as from the Lord the Spirit.

V: With unveiled faces reflecting as a mirror the glory of the Lord.

R: We are all being transformed into the same image, from glory to glory.

V: Glory be to the Father, and to the Son, and to the Holy Spirit.

R: We are all being transformed into the same image, from glory to glory, even as from the Lord the Spirit.

V: Being transformed by the renewing of your mind. (Romans: 12:2)

R: That you may prove what is the good and acceptable and perfect will of God.

V: Our citizenship is in heaven. (Philippians 3:20)

R: From where also we wait for a Saviour, the Lord Jesus Christ.

V: Who shall fashion anew the body of our humiliation.

R: That it may be conformed to the body of his glory.

V: The Lord is with you.

R: And also with you.

Let us pray:

O God, who before the passion of your only-begotten Son did reveal his glory on the mountain; grant to your servants, that in faith beholding the light of his countenance we may be strengthened to bear the cross and be changed into his

likeness from glory to glory, through the name of Jesus Christ our Lord. Amen.
(Adapted from the 1928 Book of Common Prayer Revision)

Almighty Father, whose blessed Son our Saviour was transfigured as he prayed on the mount in the presence of his chosen disciples; grant that we your children and servants, always beholding and reflecting the vision of his glory, may be transfigured more and more into the likeness of his life, and by the working of his Spirit our minds may be renewed to a more perfect knowledge and fulfilment of your holy will, through the same Jesus Christ our Lord. Amen.

V: The Lord be with you.
R: And also with you.
V: Let us bless the Lord.
R: Thanks be to God.

The Grace

The grace of our Lord Jesus Christ, and the love of God and the fellowship of the Holy Spirit, be with us all, evermore. Amen.

After the office has ended, any of the following prayers may be added:

Almighty and everlasting God, whose blessed Son revealed himself to his chosen apostles when he was transfigured on the holy mount, and amidst the excellent glory spake with Moses and Elijah of his death which he should accomplish at Jerusalem: grant to us thy servants that, beholding the brightness of thy countenance, we may be strengthened to bear the cross, through the same Jesus Christ our Lord. Amen.
(Scottish Prayer Book)

O God, who on the holy mount didst reveal to chosen witnesses thine only-begotten Son wondrously transfigured

in raiment white and glistening; mercifully grant that we, being delivered from the disquietude of this world, may be permitted to behold the King in his beauty, who with thee O Father, and thee O Holy Ghost, liveth and reigneth, One God, world without end. Amen.
(American Prayer Book)

O God, who on this day did reveal from heaven to the fathers of both the Old and the New Testament thine only-begotten Son wondrously transfigured; grant, we beseech thee, unto us that by doing such things as are well pleasing unto thee we may attain to the continual contemplation of his glory, in whom thou didst declare thy Fatherhood well-pleased, through the same Jesus Christ our Lord. Amen.
(Translated from the Sarum Missal)

O God, who in the glorious transfiguration of thine only-begotten Son did confirm the mysteries of faith by the witness of the fathers, and by the voice that came down in a cloud of light did wondrously signify beforehand the adoption of thy sons, vouchsafe of thy mercy to make us fellow-heirs of the glory of the King himself, and grant that we may share together that same glory; through Jesus Christ our Lord. Amen.
(Translated from the Roman Missal)

Christ our God,
you were transfigured upon the mountain
and showed your disciples your glory
as they were able to bear it:
kindle your everlasting light upon us sinners
by the intercession of the Mother of God.
Amen.
(A Collect from the Eastern Church)

References

Chapter 1

1. Morna Hooker, *The Gospel According to St Mark*, London 1991, p. 213
2. Timothy Ware, *The Orthodox Church*, 1963, London 1993, p. 231
3. C. F. Evans, *St Luke*, London 1990, p. 413
4. A. M. Ramsay, *The Glory of God and the Transfiguration of Christ*, London 1947, 2nd ed. 1967, p. 62
5. A. M. Ramsay, *Be Still and Know*, London 1982
6. Ibid., p. 61

Chapter 2

1. David Hill, *The Gospel of Matthew*, London 1978
2. G. Kirk, *The Vision of God*, London 1931, p. 101
3. M. Hooker, *The Message of Mark*, London 1983
4. Eusebius, HE III, 39
5. Ralph Martin, *Mark: Evangelist and Theologian*, Exeter 1972
6. C. E. B. Cranfield, *The Gospel According to St Mark*, Cambridge 1959, p. 12
7. Eusebius, HE III, 3.1,4
8. Michael Green, *2 Peter and Jude*, Grand Rapids 1983
9. J. Kelly, *A Commentary on the Epistles of Peter and Jude*, London 1969
10. P. N. Harrison, *The Problem of the Pastoral Epistles*, 1921, p. 12
11. E. I. Robson, *Studies in the Second Epistle of St Peter*, 2nd ed. Cambridge 1945, p. 49
12. E. Hennecke and W. Schneemelcher, *New Testament Apocrypha*, Philadelphia/Cambridge 1965, new edition Vol. I 1991, Vol. II 1993, p. 685

Chapter 3

1. T. A. Burkill, *Mysterious Revelation. An Examination of the Philosophy of St. Mark's Gospel*, New York 1963, p. 153
2. R. H. Stein, 'Is the Transfiguration (Mark 9:2–8) a Misplaced Resurrection Account?' in *Journal of Biblical Literature* 95 (1976): 85
3. C. H. Dodd, *Parables of the Kingdom*, London 1935, p. 53
4. J. D. G. Dunn, *Christology in the Making*, London 1980, p. 47
5. G. B. Caird, 'The Transfiguration' in *Expository Times* 67 (1955): 291
6. Vincent Taylor, *The Gospel According to St. Mark*, London 1966, p. 386
7. Bruce Chilton, 'The Transfiguration: Dominical Assurance and Apostolic Vision' in *New Testament Studies* 27 (1980): 117
8. A. Farrer, *A Study in Mark*, London 1951, p. 111
9. Ramsey, 1947, op. cit., p. 9
10. Ware, op. cit., p. 170
11. G. H. Boobyer, *St. Mark and the Transfiguration Story*, Edinburgh 1942, p. 69
12. Margaret Thrall, 'Elijah and Moses in Mark's Account of the Transfiguration' in *New Testament Studies* 16 (1969): 305
13. Ibid., 305
14. A. E. J. Rawlinson, *St. Mark*, London 1925, p. 118
15. B. W. Bacon, *The Beginnings of the Gospel Story*, London/ Newhaven 1909
16. Chilton, op. cit., 118
17. H. Riesenfeld, *Jésus Transfiguré*, 1947, p. 251
18. J. B. Bernadin, 'The Transfiguration' in *Journal of Biblical Literature* 52 (1933): 181–189
19. A. Kenney, 'The Transfiguration and the Agony in the Garden' in *Catholic Biblical Quarterly* 19 (1957): 449
20. Boobyer, op. cit., p. 55
21. O. Cullmann, *The Christology of the New Testament*, London 1967, p. 284

Chapter 4

1. A. M. Hunter, *The Work and Words of Jesus*, London 1973, p. 66
2. David Hill, *The Gospel of Matthew*, London 1978, p. 39
3. Riesenfeld, op. cit.
4. C. Kopp, *The Holy Places of the Gospels*, London 1962
5. Ramsey, 1947, op. cit., p. 113

6. Boobyer, op. cit., p. 75
7. R. Tasker, *Matthew*, London 1961, p. 165
8. L. Sabourin, 'The Biblical Cloud. Terminology and Traditions' in *Biblical Theological Bulletin* 4 (1974): 307

Chapter 5

1. Ramsey, 1982, op. cit., p. 70
2. Riesenfeld, op. cit., p. 290
3. I. H. Marshall, *The Gospel According to Luke*, Exeter 1978, p. 382
4. G. Delling, Article on day (ἡμέρα) in *Theological Dictionary of the New Testament* 2, pp. 943–953
5. Ramsey, 1982, op. cit., p. 64
6. I. H. Marshall, *Luke: Historian and Theologian*, Exeter 1970, p. 209
7. J. Manek, 'The New Exodus in the Books of Luke' in *Novum Testamentum* 2 (1957–58): 8–23
8. Marshall, 1978, op. cit., p. 384
9. Cullmann, op. cit., p. 275
10. Ibid., p. 290
11. Marshall, 1978, op. cit., p. 380
12. Ramsey, 1982, op. cit., p. 66

Chapter 6

1. Gerald O'Mahoney, *Praying St. Mark's Gospel*, London 1990, p. 64
2. R. Bultmann, *Theology of the New Testament*, New York 1955, p. 27
3. R. H. Stein, 'Is the Transfiguration (Mark 9:2–8) a Misplaced Resurrection Account?' in *Journal of Biblical Literature* 95 (1976): 79–96
4. Riesenfeld, op. cit.
5. J. A. Ziesler, 'The Transfiguration and the Markan Soteriology' in *Expository Times* 81 (1969): 263–268
6. Boobyer, op. cit., p. 4
7. Ibid., p. 55
8. R. P. Hanson, 'The Doctrine of the Trinity' in *New Fire* 8 (1984): 9
9. Norman Anderson, *The Teaching of Jesus*, London 1983, p. 183
10. Cullmann, op. cit., p. 155

Chapter 7

1. In Ruth Burrows, *Through Him With Him In Him*, London 1987
2. J. W. C. Wand, *Transfiguration*, London 1967, p. 69
3. Lewis Radford, *The Transfiguration of Our Lord*, London 1937, p. 27
4. Ramsey, 1982, op. cit., p. 69
5. Austin Cooper, *Julian of Norwich*, Homebush 1986, p. 75
6. Ramsey, 1982, op. cit., p. 63
7. Wand, op. cit., p. 70
8. Thomas Merton, *No Man Is an Island*, Tunbridge Wells 1955, p. 155

Chapter 8

1. A. R. C. Leany, *A Commentary on the Gospel According to St Luke*, London 1958, p. 112
2. Hunter, op. cit., p. 116
3. Ramsey, 1982, op. cit., p. 64
4. Radford, op. cit., p. 5
5. C. Bulley, *Glimpses of the Divine*, Worthing 1987
6. Cooper, op. cit., p. 77
7. S. H. Hooke, *Alpha and Omega*, London 1961, p. 140
8. In Bulley, op. cit.

Chapter 9

1. Hoskyns, *The Fourth Gospel*, London 1947, p. 149
2. Burrows, op. cit., p. 27
3. Ibid., p. 27
4. Marshall, 1978, op. cit., p. 383
5. C. K. Barrett, *The Gospel According to St. John*, London 1975, p. 44
6. Cooper, op. cit., p. 76
7. Ibid., p. 77
8. Wand, op. cit., p. 78
9. O'Mahoney, op. cit., p. 68

Chapter 10

1. Radford, op. cit.
2. Words and music by Dave Evans, Thank You Music 1986

Index